T0095049

The Whirling White Light
Ride in Heaven

The Whirling White Light
Ride in Heaven

Greg Belter

iUniverse LLC
Bloomington

The Whirling White Light Ride in Heaven

Copyright © 2013 by Greg Belter.

All rights reserved. No part of this book may be used or reproduced by any means, graphic, electronic, or mechanical, including photocopying, recording, taping or by any information storage retrieval system without the written permission of the publisher except in the case of brief quotations embodied in critical articles and reviews.

iUniverse books may be ordered through booksellers or by contacting:

iUniverse LLC
1663 Liberty Drive
Bloomington, IN 47403
www.iuniverse.com
1-800-Authors (1-800-288-4677)

Because of the dynamic nature of the Internet, any web addresses or links contained in this book may have changed since publication and may no longer be valid. The views expressed in this work are solely those of the author and do not necessarily reflect the views of the publisher, and the publisher hereby disclaims any responsibility for them.

Any people depicted in stock imagery provided by Thinkstock are models, and such images are being used for illustrative purposes only.
Certain stock imagery © Thinkstock.

ISBN: 978-1-4917-0692-3 (sc)
ISBN: 978-1-4917-0693-0 (ebk)

Printed in the United States of America

iUniverse rev. date: 09/10/2013

Dedicated to our wonderful Lord and Father God, and
to mention the Virgin Mary, for all of their undying devotion to
each and everyone of us.

Foreword

Even if we feel unknowing as to exactly when we will pass on over inside of the softly glowing beautiful eternal light into heaven, there is no reason not to believe that we can have valuable spiritual insight. Let God take control of your entire soul. He will lift us up in spirit while accompanied by the Lord and their glorious angels of the light. So far beyond natural belief, prepare yourself for the ride of your life. Heaven is coming right up. Just when you thought there would only be one way of rising above, straight up through a heavenly tunnel filled with the spirit flowing in such grandiose style, that which is there to beautify, without notice the Masters of light are able to pleasantly surprise the most experienced diviner.

Taken away at a moments notice is what happens to us when our time has come to an end. We are torn apart from our loved ones, yet we have a new life of eternal life, rejuvenation of our health to where we were once very youthful in appearance. Small spiral white clouds of whiteness approaches near. Is it really clouds coming in from the other side of life, or was that God's fascinating spiritual vision of holy light in formation of some sort? The beginning of a light arrangement in two separate views came to pass. It is time to explore the heavenly realm above. Out of the body is what takes place while small sparrows are singing with the heard joyous tweeting outdoors. The aforementioned white cones of very smooth white light spreads across in usable air space to bring attention to the happenings in the spirit world. Two very upright and seemingly glorified angels are pointing their ruffled wings up, while resting across from each other on a long and narrow pathway of white light which reaches more astoundingly in heaven. The golden halo crests that crown them so beautifully are a stunning masterpiece. Holding them in place is a feat in itself.

The scenery is very vivid without distortion of any kind. A yielding conscious mind with the assistance of the holy spirit goes hand in hand with such great identification. The angels watch over the spirit world for the King. The Lord will always follow us through life. A tall gold cross is being shown in heaven and the word "painful" appeared within dark lettering. The Lord feels such matters as these being told outright from the interpreter need to be proven in such a way to get a very truthful meaning across.

The angels are smiling twins. Both have golden curls of lengthy hair. Such beautiful soft brown eyes are to be admired. The Lord's creations are superb. Softly the golden hues from candles in the heavens are in the foreground of the spirit land, but only one stood out amongst the rest. It was slender and pearly white, flame and all. The Holy Bible sat before this special candle with such a smooth light all around it with a peaceful glow beneath and close to the pages golden edge. Spirit light of baby blue color are becoming clearer as deep valleys inside of the vast heavenly spirit world surprisingly brought forth golden rocky mountainous cliffs, which could almost be mistaken as majestic castle walls with pointed and very well sculptured structure. Instructed to take a look at the light, by the Lord pointing out that it is shedding itself upon the gold walls of rock is telling from the pictorial vision. Carrying on with the out of body experience is a must. Picture yourself being lifted up to the Lord by golden white angels glowing. Pleasantly they'll be smiling with you. First upon your arrival to heaven your life expectancy will be announced just by knowing that the Lord is loving and caring enough to welcome you into an eternal presence of life. Everything will be of splendid atonement. Jesus has the great reward waiting for His children as they have arrived, young and old. Somehow in spirit the Lord is trying to explain outright, while visiting Him now, that our next life will also be in Father God's hands. You're experiencing a higher degree of explanations from Him right now.

A white gate has swung open on each side of the heavenly path. You can see for miles. Even though the gateway is presently visible, the gate in itself has divided and is visible up in heaven with large swirls of pearly white music notes attached as a creative design. Peace is at hand. Jesus is pointing to several spots where He made small white puffs of white light remain still. It was still magic. He will do so much more. This is only a meeting. The Lord is especially happy to have you on His side. If you relax you'll know the real reason why you were brought here. While expecting to see perhaps a few brightly colored strewn flowers upon the path, two individual daisies on a right, forty five degree angle, they are decorative in the heavenly light. What comes as a little bit of surprise is someone kneeling down, sobbing before us. With hands covering his or her face it is easily understood that spirit people here are very empathetic. But how can this person's hands look so beautiful without any noticeable signs of aging? That was a lady who stands tall now. She wears a white carnation upon the right side of her very light colored robe. She understands the way you feel about losses in life. Overall she remains very jovial, and as her face is beautiful, now that she has uncovered her face, it is jaw dropping how pure and holy she is in appearance. Her shoulder length light brown hair would remind you of the Lord with His. Almost a match. She is a helper in a big way. She has taken a kneeling position upon the pathway which has a magnificent and very huge circle of glowing white light from up above, that's beaming down upon her. Obviously the Lord is resting upon His soft throne as He basks in the white light, which He is covered in at the present with the tinted golden glow flourishing beneath Himself. Pretty cool indeed. A sparkle of gold comes to light on the right of the two. The woman in the spirit is displaying smaller flowers such as softer violets and red flowers. Heaven is a place where it is possible to receive them. She appears to be very much in the kneeling position still while gently reaching forward and around herself to gather and place the flowers here and there, and a few to be brought with her inside of a small basket, where daisies are draped together over the edge. The Lord is visibly seen whisking her away back up into the light. On a long soothing path of the great afterlife. What you wouldn't give to keep your eyes glued on the light. It shall come. Remember that you are never a burden to the Lord.

There is a great castle in the sky where you are welcomed to stay at for eternity. The Lord is holding a small gold cross in His hand, and He wants us to know that He is very excited about offering that as a special gift. Soft chairs one would almost believe where created from white puffy clouds and spiritual light are quite the item to see, touch and feel after our arrival. Loved ones are conversing back and forth with each other while in their comfort zone, resting upon them. Not driven around, but they may glide through heaven while remained sitting.

Only the Lord's face and hair are full of a gusty white whirl wind of light right now, unless you want to count the hand size white cloud beneath His feet. He is that big. All good things come in the Lord as He has decided to let sunlight glow upon His chest. We will be able to look up inside of the heavens and be able to see and feel sunlight. It's a given. They believe in heaven, your conscious level will be raised to many different levels of enlightenment filled with joy and happiness. Dark rocks in the light now have gushing waters traveling over them into sparkling gold and silvery water waves, that comes from bulging waterfalls in the setting. Arching gold and pearly white bridges are nice to visit as they too are nearby.

You are allowed to swim in cleanliness in these waters of life. People are now seen doing this there, as the Lord dressed nicely in His white robe, He has someone very close to Him preparing to be baptized, while standing knee deep closer to the water's edge. Jesus has His hand resting upon the man's forehead, and an arm around him as much care is taken while bending down into the water. The joyful experience is for all. The man's hair appears to be wet and thick. When he came up from being under the holy water is when it was fully known. He went to his knees, first thought to be pleading to the Lord for mercy. Only because the look of desperation came across through the expression of his daunting brown eyes. A semicircle of glowing white light instantly covers the top of the man's head. He grabs hold of the Lord's robe, now wrapping his arms around Christ's legs happier than ever. The man was no longer agitated.

Why all of the red apples everywhere in the spirit? The Lord's flat hand which reaches out to His children with now a single ripe golden apple is why it came to light. As the apple was turned a chunk had been bitten out from it. The fruit is very fresh and pure. There are many privileges in heaven and one of them pertains to eating fruit. The Lord brought that up in the visual contact with Him in a higher state of existence. If the Lord's throne wasn't just now richly embellished in gold at the curled back arm rest in the front of it then that mighty throne would belong to God or the Virgin Mary. We shall see. The spirit frolics in the light almost to be singing while stepping on. The Lord's face appears. But He is bigger than ever. Very big indeed. Make no mistake about it Jesus is the happiest you'll ever know Him to be. The joyful smile from a loving King. Two tall and more imperial like gold shields with three long swords stand upright now. Vibrant palm trees come about in the background. We are in paradise. The Lord is standing a distance away surrounded by the white peaceful light that makes everything feel alright. Jesus is watching from His right side directly at us during this moment which He has chosen to be special. The features of heaven you will enjoy. People you have lived with in the past, including family members will be the first ones to embrace you when arriving. Fancy golden, silver, and bronze fire burners which are tall and slender in spherical shape are glowing gold flames of light. A young boy is peeking into one while holding on to the front with his hands. Part of the youngster's face is glowing in soft gold light, as the left side is absorbing white light from the spirit. To be funny he stuck out his tongue. Not at all a bit surprised by the lad. And he is chuckling about what was seen. He even placed his own hands up to his mouth as to be holding back intense laughter. He is quite the charmer and on the cute side. He wanted to show us more, but he was hesitant. He bows forward revealing a full head of darker brown hair. Even while visible around holy light he still looked human, but as a spiritual child in God's eyes.

In any event the boy proved he wasn't harmed, yet he was amused by the flickering flame of light before him.

Only to continue with what is thought to be right. We are being lifted still to find out what treasures await us. Even though three fingers and dark hair standing up from the top of a Indian woman's braids stand out, they're trying to tell us, that the Lord knows the number of hairs upon us. Not only just three, but it was to remind us of what He meant. People are all over the place smelling small bouquets of vibrant flowers in their hands. But everyone is covered in a serene white light, where there facial features are undisclosed for a change. Not a secret society, but a peaceful race. Not to be out of line, but a swami wearing a black spiral turban hat is present with a small quarter size glowing ball of white light glowing from the center of it. His face comes in clearly too. A long face. Firstly a fully opened red flower with very wide petals floated in front of his left shoulder blade, and the spiritual experience of his higher self wouldn't be complete without the two yellow tulips he was enjoying. He rests upon soft spiritual light with his legs folded as he grows with a strength which he believes comes from prayer and meditation. The swami's hands press together making the fingertips to both hands touch evenly. His smiling face is of peacefulness found within. He is of sound mind. He shows words. We should meditate to release the intensity inside of our brain and our body, though he leans way over to the right to be showing that's not the case with him and the people on the other side. The flexibility demonstrated is quite remarkable. By his actions he communicates we can exercise all day in heaven if we want to. As loose as a goose. The peace is so believable at best. A lot of real peace.

The holy spirit will immediately remove areas in which we think that are harmful to us and to others. We will have knowledge of the wrong, but pureness of thought will supersede that which is troublesome. That shall come from a secret method our Father uses to make us whole in uniting with Him. Privileged information will become a useful spiritual tool. You will have the ability to become visible, and then invisible to your friends on earth, after the natural passing of your life. In heaven friendly spirits are visiting one another, however, they'll disappear in a flash, not rudely because of the cordialness of their ways will be understood. We have decision making ability and that's very much honored in heaven.

Three Indians in white light are hilarious. Two whom are very tall have to be the elders of the smallest. The little girl has long brown braids, and she was the only one who stepped outside of the "covering" of white light to reveal herself more. Indian reservations are in the light where everyone can visit unusual tribes of people. It is an honor to learn their language and study their lineage. This is a sworn truth be known to all from the Indian guides who point to the tepees inside of the spirit land. They know of us and await our visit with them. Small children are peacefully touring heaven while wearing softer white angelic robes that fit them perfectly. They truly are darling angels themselves. While their eyes are set on a happy King, our Lord Jesus, the children carry small gold crosses, some that have glowing white around the edges mixed in. Being able to see is a blessing in itself, but on the other side of life you know you've been chosen special by the Lord to be with Him forever and a day. Jesus is a kind soul.

He is demonstrating the youthful side of Himself. Believe it or not there is a silver fish hanging out of the side of a woven basket, that which is carried over His right shoulder. Wow! Now He has at least a dozen slender fish with their heads popped up and out of the basket in plain sight. How could they be dead? Jesus takes one in His hand and places it in the bluest river you can imagine. It was given life. But the river looked very far away, while the Lord was just no more than fifteen feet from the interpreter. That explains how He can be everywhere, thus near and far away. You would expect that from a Grand King who can do all feats of magic. The basket is empty now. But before it became that way a fast moving wiggling activity took place in the water. Close up just like at the movies. The Lord even feels it was a better explanation than with someone who was being untruthful. He has a way about expressing the things that have true meaning in life. He has informed you of many things to come.

The perfected heavenly tunnel is covering the Lord's face, but many in heaven right now can see His long hair behind the circle of light. Without any trickery a miniature poppy flower is visible, then over away from that a blue sort of haze drew immediate attention. That gives you the feeling not only is there creation from the Lord being presented, here and there at any given moment, but He is in command of spirituality everywhere. Granite, the spiritual kingdom is full of heavenly bliss. Four pairs of specific saffron wings are seen. Then two very small and oval twinkling gold eyes appear for each one of the four angels moving forward. They've changed to show they're sporting arched ivory ruffled transcendent wings, which shows they have a mysterious secondary set adjoined. The smoothest pink new sign of an angel joins on in with the group. This pretty angel has a full crested ivory halo with a few large gold stars embedded inside. The four smaller angels are in close attendance with the bright pink angel messenger, almost as if they were in daily worship. Their obedience to one another is really fascinating.

All of the angels are singing joyfully unto the Lord. How is that so? Their peanut shape mouths gave them away, but without being insensitive to those who cannot hear, this is what it feels like not to be able to hear them sing, while out of the body with a higher conscious and visual awareness, when not being able to hear the cherubs as they sing so heavenly, while here on earth at the same time. Two places and on the money. A very wide row full of children dressed in white robes, along side of ivory and white wing angels, one person and then an angel next to them, all are bowing down before God and the Lord, except for one boy. He is actually whispering into the angel's ear, and come to find out, the Lord appears within the angel as He turns around to reveal Himself. So, the Lord is on the throne too. The Lord's angel was bowing down with Him and the special flock just moments ago.

Variations of black and blue striped lines were just shown in wide patterns laying flat on heaven's floor. A very nice walkway, which is only one of trillions. A smiling curly haired blonde gal about five and a half feet tall is standing directly behind a child's highchair, where two gold jars of baby food sit on the tray. She is able to offer the small ones food in the light, believe it or not it is so. She is hand feeding a child right now. The small child has a very noticeable frosty white halo. The child's eyes are the roundest and the bluest, they glisten so. It was funny how the child turned to the side to be noticed more. The little boy still in the highchair raised his right hand up in the light. He is not five years old, but the child acknowledges well who is visiting inside of this out of body experience, and especially where we are at the moment. The caring young lady and the child have started journeying into the light much deeper. It's strange how from a distance away in the spirit world the two are still visible.

White cloudy light is beginning to move counterclockwise around the special tunnel, but the collage of such great beauty will remain angelic with little kids with their wings while gazing up. They're floating inside and outside from the tunnel, but they are loving it you shall know. A few toot their small slender horns. Soft white and golden trumpets that fit perfectly to their lips. Small darting lines of colorful light shoot out from the trumpets, which matched the instrument. Gradually the cloudy light above them drapes the tunnel, radiating itself upon the baby angels to bring them into the light more. Not blurred vision at all, in fact the children who come as cherubs are so vivid, all human contact with them right now is from beyond the earthly level.

The Virgin Mary with Her stunning diamond studded thick silver crown worn so magnificently feels it should be explained that Her presence being known will only provide helpful insight. She has at least four small babies in Her arms. They're dark and light haired babes clothed in white garments. The children have a lot of beauty in them. The Lord says, "My Mother loves children." He communicates in our presence with spoken words visible to the naked eye, and as we live in heaven in the future, His and Mary's voice will be heard out loud. Mary has such long curls of shoulder length brown hair. Look upward for sparkling blue eyes. You can't see them? Look again until you do. Try a quick prayer to see Her eyes. You may see the infants in her arms when She appears. Mary isn't a stranger to anyone. It takes faith and a simple prayer. The heavens are all around us right now, there for the asking. Two black roses are separated by a white flower in the center held onto in Mary's hand. Sparkling gold crystals of light cover the flowers from a gleaming light that surrounds Mary now. Interestingly the Virgin Mary's robe is an enriched cream color. Her attire does change. She is nose to nose with one of the babies in Her arms. Speaking gently and most lovingly about how much She loves and cares for the child. The back of one of the infants reveals shoulder length brown and wavy hair, most likely from a baby girl, whereas, she was brought in for a better view. Mary's rosary is of ivory pearls or beads, it's a little hard to pinpoint, however there are various small green and ivory looking leaves laced.

It is kind of hard to believe that the huge Holy Bible wide open sitting in front of Mary's ivory throne is as big as it is. Apparently She has been reading the word. We can't imagine all of the fun She has in heaven. It all begins with the Lord and His Father. Mary will be a close companion too. A lamb with a gold star above him bobs up and down as to be displaying how happy he is. How very exciting. A small girl with long dark hair is patting the lamb on the head. The little girl is closer to ten years of age. A small black bow is being adjusted over her head by a lovely lady who is leaning over the child now. The happy soul is a helper in the holy spirit. One at a time, the helper points up fingers from one hand, as to be counting, and as that unfolds a small ball of white glowing light appears above each finger. The globe of earth was shown. She is relating that our days on the planet earth are numbered. That makes one pause a little bit. She left in a hurry with the child and the lamb.

Golden light is glowing beneath a number of cotton like clouds right now. If you ever wanted to have some space of your own this would be it. How very beautiful in the spirit it has become. Your comfort is desired here in heaven. Do not be afraid. The colorful clouds in heaven are non-toxic. Many clouds in the background of heaven are pink, orange, baby blue and even saturated shades of purple. Mint green clouds surface so the coloration of them doesn't completely stop just right there then. Flat hands to the side and beneath a mixed cloud filled with vibrant colors, that being of orange, white and yellow, had been patted down firmly between them. The colors became more solid, rather than bright. The cloud slowly drifts from the Creator's hands and forms three separate clouds, one of each color. A sparkling gold crown with soft points is shining upon our Lord's head. First He was smiling with a very handsome look on His face. Then the Lord began to frown, but He shows no hatred. He went from certain degrees of frowning though. As if He tried to tell people in the land below, on our side, to walk with Him and stay out of trouble. He was looking downward when the deepen frown came, and His long dark eyelashes had dropped with closed eyes for the moment.

People think it's true. You know why? The Lord said so. Yes, He is preparing a special place for His children while being entertaining. He is facing people back and forth from one to the next, whether it be a man, woman, or child who has entered the kingdom. The Lord lets the chosen people know He has been waiting. We believe that the Lord and God Almighty instantly cures us from our ailments in the spirit. The Lord takes away a man's crutches and crumbles them into many fractured pieces, and that puts a smile on a tired man's face. It was likely the man didn't arrive up in heaven with the pair, but inside of the holy vision, while visiting the other side of life, the image of the miracle taking place was more indisputable. The blonde man is amazed by the miracle. And he just can't wait to be with his family again. He was rushed by family members where there were two super huge white lilies, standing, erect nearby the group of well-wishers. But the family of overzealous people must of had somewhere important for him to go and see now. It is a common thread to be visiting with loved ones, especially in settings that surpass the norm. It's Spring in heaven. If you want a grand palace it is yours. A cottage may be granted unto you, as you wish. Inside of a large golden hand you can see a golden palace. That's right, visible within the Master's hand. That is how the Lord and our God create such splendor.

A beautiful tan horse has some turquoise light touching the two nasal passages. The horse is in the light is why. They have a spiritual way of survival. A gentlewoman rider who is in full dark riding gear starts to go away with the very showy horse galloping ever so lightly, to be parading about. Someone, perhaps God is viewing them, as a friendly spirit with quite the regarded amount of curly long golden hair. His beard and mustache glisten in gold light, but the Lord with His darker hair features is standing next to Him, therefore without a word spoken, it's hard to think otherwise than our holy Father being present. Why wouldn't you know it? He has a small ivory angel noticeably behind both shoulders, arched upward in the light. Still a very interesting mystery, whether or not it was Him at all, and not a follower of Christ.

Not to be overlooked now, the tan horse with the gleaming silver bridle, and smooth white star on her forehead, surprisingly did have a glowing gold cross embellishment on her blanket. Her huge brown eyes led you to her inner soul where she seemed to be telling one, who she was. There are children in soft orange spiritual light sitting upon horses of their own to ride. They wait patiently as their instructors stand by their side, about all ready for the children's riding lessons to begin. The instructors hesitate to move forward, so that you would have more knowledge of them on the other side of life with what's really happening. From one mind to another.

A man walked up to a horse and flipped back the dark mane of hair on its foretop. He did so with the utmost care and affection. The friendly spirit of a man loves the horse. Even though the man was in fullness of golden light, the horse was not. But they were together in the spirit. Could it be he was visiting the animal on our earthly level while still in heaven, himself? Now the man's hands are gleaming in gold light. He is in heaven with the black and white splotchy creature. The amazing horse has golden half-circles beneath each brown eye. Sort of a nice aura for an animal to have. Apparently the horse has a good soul too. Lifting heavy people and creatures to the Lord's kingdom is simplified by bringing only the living soul.

If you prefer to marry after you have gone, you'll find someone in the light who will suit your needs perfectly. A man in a black suit and tie is marrying a woman, who is dressed in a white wedding gown, right now. In the spirit above and beyond the Lord is motioning with His lips moving and actually with the Bible open in His hands, vows. They would like to become one in God again. The man and woman turn to the side to show a three layer white wedding cake with a bride and groom sitting on top. Somehow the kiss was missed out, but feel self-assured, they must have slipped that by us. The scenery changes fast, but it becomes more than just a small glimpse of what people are doing. The bride flaunts a pretty sparkling diamond on her hand. She has a soft hand, resembling flesh in the spirit. It pleases the Lord, them coming together as one. The Lord is very festive. From the bottom of the floor, to the middle of the room, and to the top of the ceiling, look for a white sleeve and an elbow. When any formation of white appears it was likely because of the Lord revealing Himself. Actually a lesson from the Master of light.

Funny, the tunnel of white light is glowing, brighter and brighter again, and beneath its origin a man cometh to it through the dark night filled with shining stars. He makes it there alive. Seeing the stars in the sky when we die is not the most likely scenario on our way to heaven, especially if that it happens during daylight. For one and for all it will feel as if we were on a peaceful flight. The Lord and His Father's heart is overflowing with love. And that's why you feel as good as you do in their presence. The unexplainable feeling about heaven, and the forever mind-boggling beauty is all due to that primarily. Three daisies form a triangle. Nice at that.

The Christ child is laying in a manger with soft golden light upon Him and Mary. The Lord wanted that told after much unnecessary hesitation on the interpreter's part. Several ivory wing angels are involved with powerful golden halos which glittered endlessly. For our benefit they came in the light. Mary and Jesus were helped on their journey and they appreciated everything that was given unto them. In heaven Jesus is the messenger of good tidings. The teachings are similar to ours on earth. The study of a dark torso, lungs, and prayer hands glowing in white light tell us something. Pray for the problems that have caused grief inside of your lungs and bones. From here in the spirit to the physical world, you've heard the good news.

Primitive people who lived on earth back in the stone ages come through heaven's light to greet us. The men's hair still looks long. They turn their hands over, palms up, revealing they have no need for weapons, and that they now are humbling themselves by bowing down before the Father with an orange light covering them. They have folded their hands in prayer. And what we would call a "cave woman" let it be known that they've become much more educated in heaven. Like being in a library all of these fine people have an open book inside of their hands. The pages are very thick with dark print. One of the books tilts forward with a gold book marker about ready to slip out from the middle pages. Now just the front of the Bible was shown outright. Small amounts of white light shines from behind the Bible and over the title. The woman was showing how she went through the stages of growth in life, to where she is now. The look of confusion on her face has completely disappeared for good. Learning more about life has helped her become much more civilized. She holds both hands over her ears, that is because she can not hear us. But we know how to communicate with her in light of the situation.

Oh, she was present with her two male friends. Down below a circle of smooth with light and an image of the earth in global form is a message, from people in the light, and their Lord, that they can visit from inside of the holy light at God's command. Two tall blue candles glow of white light now. A flower girl with brown braided hair around the crest of her head comes up close to surprise. An ivory pedestal has held her utmost attention as she leans over it to take a sip from one of the very impelling streams of white light. Her white robe is pretty. There are silver flowers and a black silk bow upon the girl's floor length attire. The peaceful fountains of light even will be found to have glittering, small colorful fish swimming around in them. Some with clear water inside as well. Let the spirit of God relieve you of your problems through prayer.

A very huge ivory staircase where you can see your own image inside the shine leads up to the throne of the Lord and His Father. Without notice the throne on the right side turns all gold. There is where the Lord is at peace, gold crown and all. On the other throne, which remains in all white a small gold cross is within the spiritual setting of a wide and golden book which lays upon God's throne. That could be the Book of Life. God is mysterious to you. The dimples on the Lord's face become well-known as a sign of a happier King. Noticeable appearances of improved health in God's people is common. The Lord wants everyone to know that we would be very surprised to know what He is doing right now.

He is preparing an eventual better setting for us. He will explain later when you reach your final destiny in life. You should know what is ahead of you in other areas of the spiritual side of life, which becomes imparted. Golden sunlight is shining down upon young children, who're enjoying the gigantic carnival, where turning Ferris Wheels fill the heavens so high up they seem miles into the air. The roller coasters have yellow glowing cross bars. Many of the cars are white with swirls of black design on the side. People young and old believe they can see the best of heaven when they zoom past the glorious sights to behold. Some rides are gold with black swirls.

Not enough adventurous visions for the spoiled spiritual people on this side of life, therefore we shall seek out the kingdom of God continuously. Up here and out of the body is a spiritual ride in itself. God knows a few will doubt Him. A brunette woman holding her head down is smiling. She is happy about the fun she is having on a slide. She holds onto the outer edge of a silver slide that has dark outer railings. She went by so fast in the light through a white ball of light resembling a tunnel, in through a yellow glowing passage. She grew very excited. She came to a halt and stood up. She has a yellow glowing stick of light in each hand resembling sparklers. It's really factual that the more you believe of what is taking place, the more tuned in.

She blows a soft kiss that flows gently in the spirit. It came from her lips and the flat hand placed beneath her chin. She has a big heart. The glow sticks are sparkling still, but she had inserted them into what seems to be a couple hunks of black clay. The same woman host grabs a hold of the one and blows really hard. Her puffy pink cheeks were really puffed out. The sparkles turned to a large yellowish circle of holy light. Golden candelabrums with three frosty white candles are here too. And that's the beauty that ensues. Three saintly men with brown beards stand side by side, and the golden auras above their heads presents them as being the Lord in the middle with His two close followers, who died on the cross as well. Why is that so? Because when they slowly turned their hands over, there were smears of red blood upon them. The saints are shaking hands in very slow motion, perhaps just grasping onto one another as a sign of reverence and fellowship in the name of the Father, the Son and the holy spirit. They do make one wonder about the blood. Thank God they have turned their hands over to reveal how spotless they are now. And do you suppose the Lord made the blood evaporate? It was too far way beyond cool just to see Him perform that miracle. Jesus is covered in a golden light again, and He holds an infant in His arms, whereas the child looks over the Lord's left shoulder. As soon as Jesus held the child up in the air the adorable child grew a white aura. Over his brown head of hair it elongated. Jesus can hold many children at one time. The wonders amaze you.

People stop and chat about their many accomplishments in life. A man points his index finger up and down at the parchment that rolls out into the light. It seems he was a high achiever. And there are many accomplishments of our own that will be looked upon favorably. Because of your faith in the Lord and in God you will be raised higher up in the royal family. Rest assure that the Lord is helping you with the translator dictating. Release the spiritual gifts inside of yourself. Close your eyes and look at the colorful sparkles of eternal light that lives within your soul. Whether it is mere concentration on the sky to watch the beautiful small wonders of light shine, while concentrating at one point up and far away, or if when at peace with both eyes closed it is for sure a beautiful sight to behold. We have discovered how to find heaven right here in our own backyard. Stand or sit still and seek out the kingdom of God. Many colors of sparkling light will tickle your fancy. As for now, here in heaven, again, angels are everywhere.

One female angel has a royal blue halo, resting upon a thick curvature of darkness in the spirit. Once that the blue halo seeps into the dark area it creates lustrous swirls, making the angel's coronet of light stunning. She is gliding through a steep valley using her snow white wings to move her one place to another. For her it was a synch to travel far away, and to come back in mere seconds. The Lord's hands stretches above the golden valley of peace, where all light prevails. Baby angels covered in all white, including the small robes they wear are checking on a white tunnel, that is farther away. Their eyesight is amazing, as anyone could tell, they were in awe. They are babies, but the angels are laughing away in one particular group of three. Their wing tips touch their delicate lip. What is so funny? You'd pay top price at the movies to see these little darlings. An angel with shoulder length dark hair tilts her head while pointing to a golden glowing light. She steps in and steps out. She is solid gold, except for her very soft dark eyebrows and very beautiful blue eyes. Her hair is still drenched in gold light.

A gardener covered in a softer white light remains on his knees tending to a flower bed. But he looks up, and places a cupped hand up to his left ear. Several hummingbirds hum on by leaving a white saturation light, to natural colors nature has given them. A yellow hummingbird is hovering over a very deep blue large flower with a white center. A red cardinal and a green hummingbird come to visit.

Three blue jays perched on white branches on a forty-five degree angle are also enjoying paradise. The words "funny person" appeared in bold black print right above them. Their communiqué was quite amusing. Visible in heaven is an owl with glassy yellow eyes He is perched on a thick brown branch, while his buddies, the grey and white cockatoos take turns bowing. Oh, just as sweet as can be. The heavenly woman who has blue eyes, and brown locks of hair to her shoulders has a canary resting upon her index finger. She strokes the yellow bird with her other index finger, being ever so fond of her pet. Their sacrament with God are just the same as humans. The canary has a brighter golden yellow light outlining the shape of its backside. That is a fact, and not just a theory. And the birds can fly.

A nicely tanned Indian seems to have only one black feather attached to his headband. The red stripe of red war paint upon his face was removed, and replaced with a white stripe. The Lord feels we should know about the changes, which were made with him and his people. The Indian guest here in heaven often searches for answers during prayer. It is a strong desire he holds dear inside his heart as his left hand is covering it now. He taps his mouth quickly, at least three times to relate he was very much, "war like" in nature upon the earthly world. He means no harm by this demonstration in the light, while hand gesturing a heart with hands and fingers curling near his chest. The guests will be many as you travel through heaven.

"It takes faith to heal on your side," the Lord says, using wording in the holy spirit. A small medical team in white light wearing lab coats is made up of two men and one woman. In heaven it is easy to understand the physical ailments, medically speaking. They are very insistent upon showing a white flower with long, but slender petals. And it is true we need to explore more with flowers. All body parts are closely examined, they should want you to know, for knowledge specifically. Several key discoveries will be made during the next twenty years. But the three on the team are not the only ones who study. While enjoying heaven, you'll always feel like you are walking around on vacation, when with family, friends, and while God and the Lord make a special fuss over everyone. The spirit people claim we are closer to a discovery in the medical field that will be beneficial for all of us in the future. We will think it is some kind of miraculous miracle. Learning will help many people become a little closer to the spirit.

Wouldn't you know it the visions in heaven just keep on coming and coming. But all the activities going on and everything they demonstrate is for real. Ripe bunches of bananas are hanging from trees in the light. But don't we know and appreciate very much what the Lord has given us in the way of fruits? True, we have. It is not impossible to eat fruit in the light. Many will say that's not true. But it is. You can grow on the other side still, and by enjoying many fruits they have given unto you in heaven, you'll feel the fruits will make you happy inside. The stomach will not growl, you'll always feel mild inside. We are taught simple lessons while in attendance of other people who have come to learn about the inner most self, which still belongs to us. An instructor is using his white pointer, which is quite long, to illustrate before a very lively crowd that the stomach and esophageal area is shaped the same, but in mere white light appearance, that which is held together within the human soul. There must be fifty people sitting inside of the group, and what is awe striking was the huge halo, that's a width of solid gold above their heads. Inside of their very own aura dome were dozens of tiny sparkling gold specs of light. They are being instructed that they would have to give up many of their habits they had on earth.

Individuals even act out some of what they were, such as a man who is very happy about sticking a cigarette into a cloudy looking ashtray. Don't worry his smoke wasn't lit. A bulging waistline and an image of a flat stomach shrinking, both covered with a white garment, proves they wear clothing, and now is the time we should listen to what they have to say about being overweight. It doesn't appear to be any heavier people in heaven. They are letting us known there should be a limit to how much we should eat while in the physical world. Back to the person with the pointer in his hand. He is pointing to the heart on a chart. Somehow another heart takes shape, bulging next to the normal heart. That would be enough to scare anyone into slowing down on their fat intake. They want us to hurry on to the next lesson. Here we go.

There is a tall tan horse wearing a black bridle, eating hay where several stacks lay. They're so fun loving that they show up more than once on our adventure. The globe of earth, the word "disabled," and a small child on top of a white horse bowing down speaks volumes of words.

A pink, white and red rose lay upon an ivory and light blue pedestal. A man in heaven has two or three nails hanging out from his mouth, with one placed in his hand about ready to be tapped into the column. But he stops, and looks over his right shoulder in wonderment. The spiritual man could easily be mistaken for a beatnik. But to our surprise, he is a builder of infinite knowledge. Build up your spiritual knowledge in the Lord. Forge ahead with your dreams. A hand grasps hold of the white rose, raising the stem up. Who's hand does that belong to? The Lord enjoys flowers. The man who is the dark mustached, bristly bearded, builder, was watching his leader enjoy Himself. Two baby boy cherubs standing effortlessly in the light are both gazing into similar white glowing hearts. One boy has brown curly hair, and the other blonde. They were too cute to be ignored. So believing and celestial. Their mild white wings extend to their side, outward to embrace each other as they seem to be walking along their way through heaven.

A jagged silver thunder bolt shoots out from the bottom of a puffy white cloud. The word "nature" was shown in dark print. God has His ways of telling us that He is not to be accused of the destruction mother nature may bring. We are not damned by Him and the Lord, we are so blessed and loved. The ball of golden light radiates a steady flow of warmth upon the Lord's hands, which are cupped together at the bottom edge. He is giving. He demonstrates a black door being penetrated by white light that left only a few dark strands of wood left. If that was what the door consisted of it was awfully artistic of the Lord. The Lord can be seen standing on the other side of the tall door, through a small arching window, inside a peaceful golden light. The window is graced by a slender wooden cross, as Jesus was occupied with us and many other people in a moment of silence. The Master of light has a creative imagination too. How He does that with many colors of light changing like that is very clever.

You'll think the fruit trees in heaven are much brighter in appearance. The many orchards cause gaiety amongst the onlookers. You are allowed to touch and sample the fruit if you desire, it is told. A lady with golden hair is pushing her hands down upon a thick white cloud of light. She has taken a seat inside. She is the center of attention right now. And she would like the ride to begin as quickly as they can get moving along. A few onlookers are out further away on the left of her, but to the right side, away from her and the ride a huge group of people in the light are very excited for a special reason. A long connection of these cloudy white cars have boarders beginning to find their place behind the woman. It appears she will control the ride. The woman has the rosiest cheeks, but then again, most everyone there glows. Up front there is a shield in the first ride, where the heavenly woman points to a guide map. It would remind you of a windshield, but with instructions across in very fine detail. The passengers are very safe and don't worry about falling out. Their hands freely hang over the side, like that with an earlier traveler in the spiritual light of kindness. There are smiles galore as the ride has already taken off in a peaceful mist of white light that still radiates above all of the men, women, and children who are having more fun than most of us right now. But we will enjoy that ride sometime after our arrival.

You might be able to dream of going on the ride in your sleep. If you pray hard enough, you won't have to wait until death before taking a very interesting ride through heaven in the light. But for now, put on your spiritual ears and learn of other people's experience of this phenomena. There is something about all of the joy that they feel that is so praiseworthy. The golden haired woman's hands are on a steering device, but only the back of her head and her hands on the wheel made it clear she was on a desirable route. Even though she was zoomed in on it doesn't mean that she wasn't any longer connected to the other passengers aboard the ride. She has made good use in what us earth people would call "travel time" as the interpreter sees her off in the distance making a huge swirl through the light. That baby can move fast. As she swishes through the heavenly white light, what's very pretty now is the holy features everywhere in plain sight, that which changed to a full ivory background, highlighting the adventure.

Everyone onboard are so friendly as the ride passes by in another realm inside of heaven. A boy with brown hair is expressing with an open mouth how surprised he is, a jaw dropping ride indeed. A couple, he with dark hair, and her with light, embrace and speak softly about how happy they are. It is read just by looking at his and her expressions. You could say they are outside with the ride entering a golden dome of light, and into a white one, and then they pass through the final channel of gold light. The handler of the long ride stands up, but she still has both hands on the wheel. If that wasn't taken place right now, then there wouldn't be a heaven. Magically the shield at the front with the route displayed turns a shiny gold. They want us not to forget that we are not forgotten, and that we are on somewhat of a ride with them. Pretty funny stuff for her to stop the ride to relate that in words and lettering visible in the light.

Someone just said, "hear." Unless he meant, "here" in the spirit. The woman in front has positioned herself with sitting comfortably again. Put yourself in the spirit as they move along. She is showing off her big white teeth. She looks over her shoulder in surprise at to what was considered to be said in kindness about her beauty. A nursery school full of angelic children come flying up to the long ride, close enough for the riders to even touch their wings, as they are now suspended in mid-light, brightening everyone's day. And amazingly enough the riders are moving about visiting golden hills that sit in the distance, but close enough to enjoy that kind beauty as well. White light softly flows upon the mountains, from top to bottom. The cherubs with their astonishing ivory wings are flittering endlessly to keep them mobile. That is a neat way to live. Many large gold stars fill in the majestic ivory backdrop. The heavens are awesome.

The golden haired beauty maneuvers the ride so that it moves around in a circle, and as that happens white light leaves a cone type impression, whipping it up to stay put in place, after circular turns. What else is there? At the top point on each cone of light a small angel with golden white wings had balanced themselves up on top with ease. And they are the tiny ones, everyone knows from the adorable golden smile on their face. A special golden light, which has spread across and behind each cherub had eventually covered their faces with exceptional beauty. Now smaller groups of golden sparkles are radiating marvelous light variations, beneath the angels from the base of the cone all of the way upward. These angels have a special halo. They are adorned by black satin, filled with sparkling silver stars. With an extended disc of white light behind them which stands out from the amazing gold light shed upon them from the Lord's hands. One of the cherubs up front has spread his wings out to fly. Now they stick straight up, which means the little boy and his angel have departed, mostly to travel up and away to go play with the children. Three angelic friends side by side await his arrival to the higher position of existence. They are a little bit ahead of the angelic boy in his travels, as the cherubs with full pink cheeks appear before he did at the appointed place of arrival. They're actually the same cherubs who were resting on top of the white cones. So, what happened was, they rushed away to an intended predestination, where they secretly knew the boy would eventually come to. Where is the straggler? He stopped to take a rest upon a sunlit ivory pedestal. A long and steady flow of golden light led him on a pathway, and before he meets up with his friends again, this is where he'll stay to observe an expansive pale purple light beneath his perch. It is regally beautiful.

A soothing light lit up the ivory staircase before a beautiful woman's throne where She reigns in power. The unbelievable amount of brown hair on top of Her head is just that. She is all smiles. Before we delve into who She is it will be explained as to who was bowing down before Her. There were not only men in front of the gigantic staircase, but there were women too. A long dark cloud fell upon all of them. But they were still clear enough to see all crouched over. Even when wanting to go on about the sinners more, a huge silver pointed crown appears. And the woman whom they bow down to is the Virgin Mary. But She is pleased about the situation, and not scornful for those who have sinned in life. Things do get better.

Before you know it white light covers each man and woman, to the point where each of them are clothed in brilliant white robes. The white Christ light has been formed over their heads, to give them that beautiful beaming crest, which resembles an aura. A small ivory cross remains with each person rising. The spirit people seem to be thanking Mary for everything in life on the other side. Their hands are folded, extended out to their Queen in thoughtful prayer and in gratitude, especially for Her Son and Father God. A new facet pertaining to Mary. Her crown has a sapphire and a red rubies on each side which sparkles grandly. Mary's people come closer upon Her request. They sit near the throne and beside Mary. A female follower with long brown hair offers Mary a colorful yellow flower. Mary lays the gift across Her soft lap. And Mary is dressed in a long white robe that has neat creases here and there in length. Out of kindness Mary strokes the woman's lovely face with the backside of Her hand. It wouldn't be heard of unless it was for the Virgin Mary's goodwill. The image of the Lord comes through the light, behind where Mary sits so high in esteem. There are more people living in heaven that know how common this type of situation is with the Lord and His Mother, than those whom live in the world.

Instantly many yellow roses drifting upon an astonishing drapery, that's just endless, very much in sight and out of sight. What a beautifully created image! Tiny yellow hearts are still glowing inside of the drapery, and a pretty woman peeks out from the inside. She grabbed hold of the drapery in the center, and one could very well see the intensity of glowing gold light in her hand. We may call it an everlasting curtain of beautifully decorated light. The nice part is the woman is smiling like a teenager, happier than ever, and believe it or not, she waves us inside as she moves from side to side while opening the curtain. Her hands become surrounded by glowing gold light, but she distances herself from everyone while she bolts away.

Three proud angels with a golden chest puffed up are people who do have faces. For good reason they are black and white, as they're very colorful, but mysterious too. It is like watching black and white television in color as well. A crazy, but very cool combination. Their white haloes are glistening with sparkling silver. Two frosted white wreaths have red berries and green leaves upon them, whereas they formed a perfect heart after moving together, without anyone's hands touching them at all. Inside of the holy spirit is where it is at. Now two thin hooks of white light made a heart, but in an entirely different fashion. After the first bending formation appeared, God and the Lord repeated the same action, but the other side of the heart made from the light which was bent over at the top, was facing the opposite direction. Then they made it happen like aforementioned earlier. They feel we should be joined together as one, and in love with the Lord. And they are personal feelings, Jesus knows all too well.

Still, the spirit insists on us feeling the need to heal our bodies on earth. But what He is demonstrating inside of the holy light are a few individuals pressing their hands to each side of their head. Press them up to your head, but don't cover your ears. Press lightly up against your temples. These three words appear from the Lord: Expect A Miracle. Stripes of golden light descending from a white tunnel of light lands at the base of the neck, with the participants who are in a healing session using the light. It does happen in heaven. A prime example of what people on our side show follow. A lady wearing a full white bonnet comes forward. She is praying as she walks gingerly.

She pointed to the tunnel of light, snaps her fingers, and a sparkle of gold touches her fingertips. Believe the Lord will heal you. From the white eternal light of wonder working power, pray to be delivered from sickness using golden rays of light.

Better to go with what they want you to know first. God wants to guide us right on through life. That's why the messages about heaven have arrived. At home on earth, and especially up in heaven, all we have to do is look down at our feet and see golden angels appear, shinier than ever. A mature woman, who is motherly, opens a silver heart shape locket, which truly does hold special and loving memories of her beloved husband on earth. She has darker hair, but a golden light covers the large braid on top of her head, leaving some dark strands visible. What is so sweet is she visits the entrance of heaven's glorious white tunnel. She looks to see if, maybe her husband is on his way to her. She knows exactly when his time will be finished in the physical world, but she enjoys peeking in on him. Also, with the locket in hand, she lifts it up in front of her face, hoping he will notice it from his side of life, where she tends to reach out to him a little.

Many people stand on the other side enjoying the warmth and love in the Lord's presence, and they, too, enjoy trying to grab their sweetheart's attention. By moving their wrist around with the silver bracelet or watch on, they'll flash it once or twice when trying to relate to our side. And you know the people on our side receive these messages and secretly know who is doing that inside of the spirit. It would be harder to believe that the settings you last resided at would be similar to that in heaven. But your house and belongings once owned may be by your side. The Lord will enhance these areas of your life and more richly. The melodies you'll be singing will be your favorites. Your intellect increases naturally. The amazing capabilities are more superior than to which we had acquired inside our homeland. And we'll be called upon to learn lessons.

Going back in forth over serious matters will no longer exist, due to the tremendous amount of balance within. The Lord understands that it is a tremendous change when passing. All fluffy white standing about six feet tall is the Lord, and the white cross being held in His left hand is a surprise, only because He had caught the interpreter off guard. You know that loving feeling you get when you see a beautiful collie being walked about? You just love that kind of dog. Jesus is our well-favored King and personal Savior for you to love the same way. He won't bite you.

Jesus is chuckling. And He is very kind like your mother and father. A huge black boulder pops up in the light. But this has more meaning to it than just sitting immovable. A white light is glowing on top. Soon it becomes a light ray, glowing straight up about one foot above the boulder, but it came from inside. Curiously a young man is sliding his hand over the light, and when that takes place, the light decreases in height and appears to be about four inches high. He is very amused, but he is questioning why it had diminished into an overflowing white light, that which continues pouring over the mysterious formation. The young man concentrating on the stone with great light, folds his hands, and rests them upon it now. He has high hopes for much happiness. He is amazed by what he sees. The white glowing light spreads across the heavens, and from where he is, and where there is an out of body visitation happening, down below we are able to see many planets, including earth covered with the spiritual light. The heavens also light up with soft yellow, baby blue, and other smaller patterns of white light in the shape of small feathers. If anything the decorative scenery is fabulous.

A serene background filled with puffy pink clouds and two large airliners glowing in mild orange light is a perplexity. Let's see what the Lord means by this. Well, the earth way down below is visible, and the fun tunnel of white light is within a coalition to the heavenly sight. There is a physical world where we enjoy the good life, and the spiritual level is that special place where the Lord uses images often to make a strong point. People are riding through heaven on flowery decorated chairs. They safely glide about to go visit their friends. It looks like a lot of fun. Both of these people are related who're journeying on the path. He has dark swirling hair, mostly covering his forehead and ears. Her hair has large rolled curls. They have a similar facial expression, and they have said they were related. You can dream all day if you want to. They tell the interpreter they are going to a wedding ceremony and to talk about the visions. And it is what they hoped for in heaven. God is above all and He is sweet inside.

The Lord was thought to have been standing next to an Indian chief. The Indian, all covered in white, wears a full headdress. But then it was time to change a point of view. Turns out the Indian chief looks like Jesus, fully bearded and a matching mustache. The only difference is that He was dressed like an Indian and completely covered in a blanket of white light. Quickly, His appearance changed drastically. The Indian is in full color. Unbelievable! You've probably never seen an Indian chief with a dark beard and mustache before. His face has a nice tan. His feathers are two-tone, per feather, white on the bottom half and black on the top. Although He does have a limp red one, slightly fallen over His face. That could be God. You just never know.

And where did that interesting giraffe come from? But there is a special helper for another animal, he who holds a chimpanzee in his arms. He is so funny. The man has a long white pointed beard, and a handlebar mustache. Not to mention the spiral white turban upon his head. He believes he can see your future. How lucky can we be? We'll be arriving unexpectedly.

A big party is going on in heaven. The mild golden light brightens just enough to where the large orchestra of men and women are in total bliss. Many of the cheerful men and women sitting before a mistral conducting a splendid symphony have the blessings of all the onlookers in their immediate presence. But with white rounded hills far away in the background, more people with a hand held close to their ear are now listening to the sweet sound of music being played. Believe it or not, the large group of people playing still enjoy following along with sheet music.

It is instilled within everyone to perform with strength and dignity. Men in such great form, standing at an angle, remain blowing out enjoyable sounds from their shiny gold trumpets. A player stops performing, only to reveal that he has a big smile on his face. The light upon him is brilliant. Two of the ladies in concert stand up and make loud clashing with their large rounded cymbals. And they are proud. Women flutists are up in front, and as their fingers move across their instrument of light, white music notes flow through the air. Inside of the crowd of people, five girls very young in age are standing out notably. All in floor length soft white robes, they're kitten soft in appearance with ivory angel wings sticking upward. A tinkling of a small bell sounds off. One of the angelic girls holds her right hand to ear, cupped. It was heard quite easily. The girls point to their hair. They have brown hair, but the shades keep getting lighter. Each girl is unique. You are to learn that they are wearing white flower wreaths upon their heads. There is plenty of spiritual air to breathe in heaven. The children are most colorful, especially with the very blush cheeks. We'll be rewarded with a freshness the same way.

Apparently the team of girls are very much a big part of the orchestra after all. They have both, hands and wings. On their wrist a band of silver bells jingle and jangle with each lively bolt from their hands reaching upward and out. The angels know a little bit that we probably haven't given much thought into. When they speak, very soft colors of spiritual light will appear. Soft glowing, but not too intense. The angelic girls are so cute, and they believe that they better help us. We shouldn't be alarmed. The presence of the Lord is with them. With ingenious thoughts running through their heads, a foaming white light behind them, now turns into, not one, but five impenetrable masses. Now the girly angels on each side are holding their index finger to their lips. What could they be trying to tell us to keep secret? Probably what is happening right now. Most people would think we were being ludicrous for believing in such guidance.

Should we keep quiet every time we receive a spiritual message, or have an out of body experience to heaven? No, that is not what they would want us to be silent over. But one angel looks menaced, and her friend is smiling. Now the two girls become very close, shoulder to shoulder, and they're giggling away like mad. There's just something eventful they don't want revealed right away. As if we haven't seen and heard quite a bit of unusual things going on up to this point. We will just have to explore more with help from the spirit people.

Like you may have already imagined there are some folks up in heaven who walk around barefooted. The white flowers grow on green stems in the gardens, where people are welcome to walk amongst them without shoes on. You'll see red ladybugs with black specks sitting upon green leaves, one on a higher leaf, and even another on a lower leaf. When all of them are in your presence of the light surrounding you, that's when you'll find the gardens look even more germfree. Because of the holiness. Insects know something very special is happening, they're that intelligent in heaven. We won't be plagued by their presence, as that sometimes happens on earth. You will think they are visually more aware, especially around plantlike. They are real characters themselves. The spirit keeps trying to say, "There is nothing to worry about."

With charcoal black mountains of great height in the background in the light, they suddenly shrink smaller and much smaller, until they become tiny. The Lord is and can move mountains, so don't be afraid to have Him do the impossible. Is the Lord running His soft hands through someone's hair right now? You'd do a double take for sure. His hands raise upward as if He were, stopping, and then going in short waves of motion with His palms face up. But you can't see anyone's hair anywhere, just the Lord's unbelievably, righteous two hands. He wants everyone to lift Him up to receive gifts. Once you worship Him, you'll be more open to receive from Him. The Lord is here in spirit. He bends over in pain, nearly touching the ground, as He is carrying a cross upon His back. He is relating in the spirit that

He knew He would be delivered. If you believe Jesus can speak to you on the other side of life, have faith that He communicates inside of your home too. The Lord believes people might distance themselves from the interpreter if told to look up into the air space, where you live, to search out words to appear like magic. But they would show in black lettering or perhaps in another color. Look for bold print, it will come. But the Lord has a valid point. Most spiritual prodigies will understand this method of communications in the spirit, given from the Lord up in heaven right to your livingroom.

Meanwhile, all of the people in heaven enjoy the feeling they receive when they move their hands up and down inside of the light. We will experience entertainers often waving their hands all about, and when they do, twirling gold light will illuminate in front of you. Once we learn how to control our feelings in the light, we'll have special privileges, such as creative design coming out from our fingertips to amaze the many onlookers.

Little children with dark hair are peeking out from inside of whirling white circles of fluffed light. Just believe that you're going to receive something big from the Lord real soon. Pink glowing light lights the inside up, where you notice the young children are in heavenly bliss with such beautiful eternal presence surrounding them in the spirit. The kids look as if they are heading down hill now. In celebration of their life the excited look on their face is obvious, the same look as the youngsters would have when seeing presents wrapped beneath the tree on Christmas morning. They spiral away unharmed by the distance they travel downward and around inside of heaven, past sparkling gold trees with silver stars. On each side of their whirling white cloud of light with that pleasant shade of pink, there are white angelic wings that stretch out. Whether the kids make believe they are riding inside of small airplanes is entirely up to them. They pass by a few people who stand away from the kids, but the onlookers still wave to them. The people paying close attention to the kids traveling into the spiritual side of life are covered in a discontinuing wall of golden light. Crystal balls of golden light shine bright as the kids enjoy the journey. They have arrived to a place, where if a kid wants to eat a white cloud that looks like cotton candy, he or she is welcome. Only God and the Lord know the true ingredients inside of the tasty treat. And with children side by side sharing a bite from these white, blue, pink and yellow whirls of cottoned candy, it is for certain they are having fun.

A streak of bright blue eternal light with an underlying white bottom to the image is part of the basic foundation at their stop. With the kid's imagination they create images, but they won't clutter their heads up with too much information, and they can leave that state of mind after searching for something else. There are many yellow, red, chocolate, lime, and multicolor suckers and lollipops just everywhere for the kids to enjoy. With the many dentists who were brought up to heaven it is very unlikely that they would need to perform any dentistry on the children. The degree of sweetness for the treats were well thought out ahead of time. Less thought will be given to the sensitivity of pain, unless you're invited to learn a special lesson involving such a feeling, concerning you and others. Endless deep valleys filled with rows and rows of the candy treats can be seen, perhaps for the young and old alike, just alone for enjoying the wonderful sight.

Three churches topped with a cross are covered in white light, and an image of the earth in global form rests nearby. Which translates into the Lord's churches are of the light, whether in the heavens or on our side of life. Christ is with us to teach many religious and spiritual experiences. It's nice to be able to see these messages while higher in a state of discernment that no one can match, unless the Lord has granted such great insight to you, that offers entitlement.

Inside of the spirit world it is impossible to lose your health. A mature woman with a swim cap on and a bare chested man, who appears to be her sweetheart, are splashing and pushing forward arm lengths of pure water to their partner. That is inside of a huge endless pool of clear water. We are entitled to such joys in life when in heaven. They also think we would be surprised by what else they do. There are stemless red roses floating in the water, floating up to the man. Amazingly he remains in focus while lifting the flower to his nose as to capture the sweet fragrance. He moves in slow motion across the water when enjoying it. While moving his face off to the side in sheer ecstacy, that's showing peace of mind. A silvery blue dash of light shines.

Tan buttons are popping up everywhere, which means you were cute as a button to your parents and grandparents when alive. If you want messages from your loved ones, ask in the spirit for them to come through. Unfortunately the people inside of the spirit world are saying that many of their loved ones they try to reach, visibly, become busy for that sort of visitation. A large "B" appears which means they also have a secondary plan for reaching you. They mean they'll contact us in our sleep with images of yesteryear, and for much needed love to be received from them. They'll go beyond to see you. And we can go far beyond this old earthly world of ours and visit with loved ones who manage to lift us up through, either the amazing white tunnel of light, or perhaps it will come in the blink of an eye and you're in heaven with them, but still fast asleep. They are telling the interpreter that they can also help you build trust in the Lord this way. See how peaceful the uplifting visitation went with your beloved?

We manage to be sitting quite still inside of the light when the Lord teaches us how to leave our body at night. But look up toward the ceiling and watch the signs and wonders begin to form. They'll roll out the red carpet for you anytime, and anywhere in time. It is definitely playtime. First imagine, if you will, a white statue standing not too far away from you now. Look away from the site where you thought it would appear. But keep that image in your mind, and hopefully the statue was that of a man or a woman dressed in a white robe. Go ahead and with your forethought, check that area out again to see if an image in all white appears. Don't look away though. Concentrate for at least a minute for a large white statue of a person to come inside of the holy spirit to greet you. There doesn't need to be a word spoken, but your's and their actions will lastly surprise. Watch for a golden aura or a crown to appear on top of the tall statue. If the light is silver it may turn into a stunning crown. The holy spirit suggests you do not be frightened by the Lord's or His Mother's appearance. Be patient and wait at least for a couple of white domes of light to come. And you will see by intense concentration that either the Lord, or Mary will come in the light, if not both of them during the same visit. That's why it's suggested by them now to look for their glowing domes of white light, first. They want you to be assisted that's why this message is coming through to you.

We're just astral traveling and having a ball. Past the stars and planets as close as can be up inside of the kingdom of God. Who comes in to greet us with a very shiny silver tray carrying a brilliantly, eye catching gold crown upon it? Two hands come in, but without a face or name it's going to be hard to say who just did that. He reached through a fog of white light that was huge in dimension. A soft yellow, orange, and a pink spreading light forms next to each other. The top of the white fog is decorated in pink. The presenter of the crown scoops it up and over to fit upon His head. And He has company. You won't believe the beautiful Mary for Her grace and eloquence. Her face is so pure. Her silver crown remains upon her head, but wait, She giggles and it has been related in spiritual terms, "wording" which She shows in bold black lettering, that Her happiness is because of the love She feels from people on both sides of life. It would be hard for any single guy to find a date as beautiful as Her. But all women should be equal still. That was just a point of view, funny as it may sound. What a living doll. Don't wait until you die, seek out the two white domes of eternal light, right before your very eyes.

Here comes a new opening inside of the heavens. Clockwise, one by one very light blue candles attached to holders with a swirling handle to hold, have formed an arc, which goes completely around in a circle. A little girl standing four feet tall has auburn hair, and inside of her cute little hand, between her fingers a white and a soft red flower were carried. She is a special guide. She wishes that we look at the change to the many candles surrounding her, as she points to each one in continuance, there is a pink color of light that surrounds the candles, as the light blue wick changed. She made that happen just by pointing her small finger at them. She is secretly relating to say something about the spirit. And she is quite polite. It's funny how her mother is leaning over her inside of the white eternal background, guiding her little one with loving hands gently resting on her shoulders. They will wait for more to be said. It seemed like her mother was ready to bring her up and further away inside of heaven, but there is more to be learned. Although both are present, behind the little girl's head a gleaming golden crown appears. She wasn't wearing the Lord's crown, but it's obvious that besides them, the Lord is very much present within our company, making all feel unified again. Why is she pointing to a brown teddy bear, and a white one, both with similar soft brown eyes? After pondering some there must be polar, and the teddy bears in the light. Now we see what she means.

In the background two huge white polar bears are hunched over, one behind the other, but not too close. They are huge in comparison to the little girl's stuffed animals. They come forward so fast you don't have time to breathe. There is some concern over the look on the first bear's face. His mouth has opened wide and his teeth are amazingly razor sharp. Is he that mean? His pal over on the left, you'd swear he was almost laughing, the facial expression is of much more to our liking. But have no fear the Lord is here. He wants everyone to know how important it has been to Him to change how the bears would act, from being a little wild, to a more peaceful creature up inside of the heavens. Mother's child points to her teddy bears as they're hopping about merrily, off to her side and then backwards. And they were joined at the paws in dance. A stunning pink ray of light beams down through the heavens, and closer to where it originates there are several merry-go-round rides turning. And guess who is riding one of the make believe ponies? The small child is with other kids. Her mom is enjoying the ride, even though she remains standing. The structure of the merry-go-round rides are bright in color. The tops are soothing yellow, while sloping above the riders. The ponies go up and down, your eyes can tell you that. They are brown, white, and silver. The ponies have a very deep and glorified sparkle. Much in silver and white combined. But as you see how bright and sparkly the ponies are they were embellished only by the keenest Masters of the heavenly kingdom. Including the shiny gold cross upon the top of the merry-go-round ride. Each pony has their own gold-plated cross as well.

The little darling girl and boy angels, you can imagine are resting in peace, some with an elbow leaning on a billowy cloud, and that wouldn't be farfetched to believe in. The kids are doing that right now. The way the angelic young kids come in so clearly is because they rest deep within the holy realm of God's heavenly home. They're so precious. What would heaven be like without them? They are up here in heaven for a reason. A golden hair boy with a ton of curls laughs about the spots of red, white and blue, that become visible beneath him. He likes to tease. Even a small white and yellow ball of light glows, blinking off and on with the others now. His wings have a fold, outwardly, very much in a ruffled and ivory manner. His blue eyes glisten. A really neat aura above his head sparkles in gold, and he makes it glitter upon his finger.

Widths of blue color are sparkling with silver stars. Three black satin pillows were pointed out by the angelic boy. At least his ivory wing dips down near them. The pillows are lightly squashed, but they are still very smooth. The pillow in the middle has a silver cross upon the covering, along side of a silver star. The other pillows were bare. But the pillows now become saturated with white light, after all. The happy boy lays his head down upon a pillow full of Godly light, then picks up the other one that matches, and he holds it up to be examined, as if he were looking inside of a mirror at himself. He turns it from right to left, shifting it around in curiosity of what might be inside of the shining light coming out from the pillow.

Suddenly a slender and very brilliant ray of golden light shot upward and out from one of the sparkles of gold on the boy's aura. It arched over him, and touched down upon the satin pillow, where the golden ray of light formed a perfect gold cross, and a larger glowing sensation inside of the white light, which had already remained in a even flow. It really is real. Talking about taking another good look at what is going on inside of the holy spirit to be right on the money. Right when we so desperately needed guidance and direction from God and the Lord, the golden cherubic lad has led the way. He knows what is best to learn from inside of the good light.

Four very white staircases are all in one big circle. There are at least ten steps to each one in close proximity. Peeking in between reveals a cloudy white light down below. It is mystical, but very spiritual. Shall we go downstairs to a lower level inside of heaven and have a look see? The Lord is in full agreement now, right here inside of the light with us. The light has flowed upward, and drifts over the very first step on each flight of stairs. People below are sitting around in the light in this deeper spiritual aspect of living, many of them with the very soft blanketing light wrapped around them, appearing to be in thick coils. Their hands are moving freely, and it is a real blessing to see their faces. Vapors of steam are uprising all around the people resting near springs of very clear silvery water, which is very rejuvenating. That's a bathing process which brings about peace. They're not smothered with the light wrapped around their souls. They are however, very much enjoying the blessings from their Supreme Master, Jesus.

Upward where the brilliant warm background of white light is decorated with a large arrangement of colorful orchids, the Lord comes in a peachy orange vibration of light. What He is doing will simply blow your mind. He is excitedly sampling the scent from a few of the lovely flowers. Jesus holds one very close to His face, and brother does He ever smile. You've never seen such happiness before, over a flower! He has many variations of blue and white orchids before Him in a full bouquet as well. There are other yellow and orange orchids which are very beautiful and are delicately appealing. Small whirls of white clouds fill the scenery, thus near and far. Balls of smoother white light have embellished the heavens in the setting too.

An arched doorway is in view ahead of us now. Two spiritual helpers stand guard at the entrance. Up close now, it's easy to understand that God's helpers want us to enter in through the doorway and we can. Even though these two people are in the light, their hands seem to be flesh color. But they are really soulful spirits still. The rest of their identity was entirely incognito, while covered in all white light. Their outline of themselves helped more. They were wearing some sort of funny white hat, pushed back. Curiously, they are looking inside of the doorway covered in white light. One of the helpers, you could see him on the right and up higher, than the other person down lower, over to the left. They're in the white light, while strongly encouraging us to take a peek inside with them. At last they're inside. It's amazing to watch them turn from the outside entryway, and to experience the two helpers step inside of a much different tone of the light. Their shoulders turn some to show they are dead serious about who they are. There is gold design everywhere it just doesn't stop. And softly heard now was a "clink" noise. The helper's heads and faces appear inside of the full white light, and a movement in the spirit world, twice, revealed the two guides were celebrating the Lord by cheering His name with their silver glittering chalices, touching each others in their toasting of Him. Taste the fruits of the spirit.

Surprisingly the helpers are two very beautiful females who reveal themselves a little bit at a time. A stripe of darkness falls upon their faces, probably just to gain more attention to what they're really doing, a self-adjustment period of some sort, which is more helpful when realizing who they are. But suddenly they have become more visible, not covered in as much white light. The ladies are holding hymn books in their hands. Now the books were still in the white light. But when one of the ladies turned the book around it was covered with lines and actual musical notes. Wording was combined.

You'd laugh your rear-end off if you saw what they were doing next. Somehow they became covered in white robes and light again. You can see their arched backs as they're down on all fours now. They look like they're ready to play football. Second thought, are they in prayer? How in the world can they bring us into a communion with them at a second's notice? In heaven that's where you can go and collaborate with all acquaintances.

No one can say that the Dutch don't go to heaven. Dutch women wearing their soft triangular hats can be seen mingling with family. Their dress wear is special. Everyone is moving hastily in the spirit. One of the Dutch ladies in the floor length black and white pattern dress on took six steps forward, and suddenly uprose, magically inside of the light, ending up inside of a warm villa, where her and a little girl stood and stared from two windows. Surprisingly there was a nice golden light behind them, and the window frames held a gleaming gold cross in place.

The outside of the villa has those castle walls in the structure. The woman inside of the window on the left presses her hands flat together in prayer. Her young one folds her hands together while in prayer. The word "believe" appeared in bold black lettering. Suddenly their windows fill with puffy white clouds, leaving them invisible, but they are somewhere inside very much enjoying their stay inside of their new villa. Beautiful raspberry color fills the heavens. A tall soft black candle with a sharp golden flame is in view. But that changes quickly with a twin. Huge rays of gleaming light shines from the wicks, rising up and far away, feeding glorious sunshine into the opening of heaven. Silver and small blue glittering lights shine magnificently. They are very tiny, but ever so meaningful. An ivory wing angel is playing her u-shape harp in front of her. How can we not believe she is doing such when her head is bowing, while concentrating on the heavenly fine strung instrument for her to play and enjoy? A glowing circle of calming gold light has been spotted on her tummy, centered right behind the harp in her arms. The strings on the harp are real, but the way they were made comes from knowledge in the hereafter, what comes from our Creator in heaven. The angel bats her eyes a little bit. She was blessed with very brown eyes, too.

A large gold key is set apart from many others which are grouped together in a ring. And wouldn't you know it the key levitates itself, now visible sidelong. The end touches a small white cloud, but how does that open it up? The key turns sideways as to be starting something on the inside. But then the key returns to its upright position, possibly already serving its purpose. The Lord's lips kiss the end of the key, because He decided to take hold of it instead of leaving it sit unattended. How important is this key to the Lord. The Lord fits the key into a hole at one of His favorite doorways, this one which has the high arching entrance. You'd think we were already inside of His glorious mansion, and we are. Again, He has many mansions in heaven. To mention "here" in heaven, would have the untrained mind a bit confused as to where and why these miraculous spiritual experiences are occurring. Understand, when we are in the Lord's presence inside of His mansion, we must respect everything He and Father God are doing. Please don't use the "shut off" switch and kill this most interesting divine experience, henceforth.

At first it seemed a little unearthly seeing an edge of smooth white light at the edge of the opening door. Yes, the Lord is ready to give us more leisure. Inside of the door stands a gigantic Fatherly figure of a man, bearded and mustached, a lot of shoulder length hair, while all covered in comforting white light. Instantly, Jesus appears, but in the same descriptive way as His Father. That has to be God with Him. Jesus secures a fixed look upward. His lips move once. One thing for sure, God is super big, supportive, and very believable once you see Him, and a Godly Father, who art in heaven is someone you'll want to be on the right side with. The God flicks His wrist, making gold light shine with a small cloud and blue sky develop. To see that happen is quite a miraculous sight. Words inside of the holy spirit read: If you believe you will know Me.

This is funny and very cute. While small yellow flags on stands are starting to pop up in the heavens, the cutest boys and girls come to visit, riding in and driving their very own little white cars that are fun for them to drive about in. They have bold black numbers on the side of each car. Variations of the colors blue and yellow bounce around in the heavens above the children drivers, decorating the background, blinking off and on in a non-disturbing way. It is a big party for the kids. There is a little boy who is talkative, but since the Lord is only allowing wording appear at the moment this is how his words will be translated inside of the light. Wording appearing read: I know your name. The little one has an amazing soft golden light caressing his blue eyes. He sees better than we do. While riding in his special car, he hangs a twirling windmill toy outside from the little convertible, to enjoy watching it turn shades of yellow and white as it moves quickly. That has to be wind or air turning the play toy. A small girl inside her car holds up three fingers. She is telling us she is very young. With dark bangs and eyelashes, she is a living doll. How in the world she got a hold of chewy bubble gum is her little secret. A pretty big bubble is forming from her lips. Not exactly big lips. The bubble is very pink and forms a heart.

Intermittent streaming golden light in the form of water shoots up into the air, cascading back to the fountain, which is presently in the same part of heaven as many of the other fountains are. Silvery glittering and foaming white flowing water is of another beautiful fountain's features. They are everywhere in the heavens with pink light beautifying many of the fountains. Baby blue background light softly glows against the high rising water fountains too.

The holy spirit took five fluffy white bird's feathers and spread them apart to create an open arrow, pointing up and down, as one feather had been added for the centerpiece. Puffy pink cheeks and a blowing motion outward lifts the white feathers up upon a small robe, that now is perfect clothing for an infant. The child's robe has been enhanced with white feathers, which fits really well. The child is laying inside of a very soft white crib. There are black roses next to the crib for an unknown reason, but one would suppose the Lord wants them there. The Lord's powerful hands, palms up again, now are raising the child up. One, two and three. Not only does the child grow, but her robe increased in size. The word "five" was shown in black letters. She even has shoulder length curls of brown hair now. A satiny white ball of light behind her head is a halo granted unto her. The strangest things happen, don't they?

When we see Jesus in heaven do these things, which remind us of amazing magic tricks we almost become envious of what He can do. Because we want to be just like the Lord. But He will teach us how to become more loving. You'll be thought as to be a very interesting person in heaven, not just the others. Get ready to feel more protected, Jesus would want that to be heard.

Up in the heavens a white tunnel, and a small whirling white light is in view. Smack dab up close a black engine for a locomotive is leaving on a black railway. A gleaming gold cross is attached to the side of the engine. There is a engineer inside who is covered in white light, but we can still make out that he is a man. Up inside of heaven, you never know if a woman is in charge of the unusual rides and entertainment indulged. The spiritual man is examining a white piece of paper now. His pink cheeks are big. First person you would think of when seeing him would be "Santa Claus." As he leaves on the track more of his snow white hair is revealed. And it's down to his shoulders. He turns quickly, looking over his shoulders to find that white light has spread across his back. He wants us to know by his actions, that bringing the white light, over our backside and upon our head, we can open the spiritual mind and eye within, not only to see in the heavens, but to experience what he is doing inside of the locomotive. A huge white sun is something you've never seen before, but this is above him. White rays of light and all. Another unbelievable sight unless you've seen it. But you can. Picture the light behind your head, using your mind, body and spirit as an open receptor. One large puff of white smoke, obviously in light form appears above the train, and many small smoke clouds trail behind.

The word "listen" appears in the holy land of heaven, but do you hear anything? A large golden bell and a silver one within in-depth perception a distance away, neither chime nor ring. It sounds like someone said, "hey." The bells have a billion small sparkles though, and sure enough a teensy ringing noise was heard, first in the right ear, and secondly inside of the left. The spiritual world is alive. The mind is beginning to boost up in a strong cognizant level higher yet.

They prefer that we magnify orange eternal light in front of ourselves, to be able to retrieve the holy visions clearly. Visualize a ball of orange color in front of you, or off on angle across the room. The orange light sheds itself from the inner layer of its holy beam, which is radiating quite heavily right now. The light expands across the room, and at the same moment it widens above and aside the tunnel of light. This is what the Lord and God Almighty are showing. You can hardly believe it unless you see it for yourself. But that doesn't mean you'll be left out from the big surprise awaiting you, upon the beautiful ride upward to the very glorious heaven in the sky. The Lord is going to relate the surprise up ahead, through using the interpreter, working as a spiritual entity for Him. Find out what He and Father God are going to bestow upon you and your family. It will be very delightful when it comes about.

Being a willing participant of visualizing the spirit's holy light glowing within the heavenly realm, it comes to you as this source of enrichment. Watch the light penetrate throughout the important aspect of the heavenly sight. It appears that dark mountains are forming in the same light. A trapper comes to visit. He is wearing a coonskin cap on his head, that is for sure. But the cap and his deerskin coat is white and very fluffy. His feet are covered in a white fabric, mostly of the light which has never been seen before, at least the softness and material left that impression. Real guns are not allowed in heaven, but the man has a very tall rifle by his side, only used as an example of how he lived when on earth. Why is he present in the spiritual out of body experience, one might wonder? To let you know his feelings about heaven.

He is on bended knee thought to be praying, but it is sort of unusual that he has his hand over his mouth, as though he were gesturing, perhaps he made mistakes in life too. Oh, now he turns his fingers more upward in front of his mouth, instead of sideways, signaling he saw Indians up close in his day. A big Indian with black feathers and a matching stripe of color across his face is standing near the trapper. They are toe to toe, looking directly at each other. But the trapper is covered in all white, while the male Indian is very much full of life and colorful. The friendly Indian tapped the trapper on his shoulder, and suddenly he too, became more full of eternal life and vibrant color. His cap is light brown with a black and white ring tail. Any ways, he is allowed to wear a racoon style cap up in heaven. He thinks we think he is fancy. The two are friends inside of the holy spirit, and it's obvious that they see eye to eye on matters.

Someone in the light is teasing us. Twice hands appeared with one on a control switch. It was a dark button on a glowing gold device, about the size of a television remote. The hands disappeared, but then came back and anyone could see that the spirit was experimenting with an off and on switch. The Lord and an unknown figure standing inside of a peach color light are full of happiness, and they're really up to something, not sneakily but thoughtful. Please do not question why the Lord keeps appearing. How would it sound if people started asking you why the Lord kept on appearing before you and your family on the other side? He sometimes uses the weak and downtrodden to get the message across. The Lord is in full control of our predestination. White spots are everywhere right now. But what might make more sense is that these small white spots in the heavens are different tunnels of white light, in the distance, whereas they may expand much wider and open for people as a special passageway, for those lucky souls who're now passing over into the light. There are many special ways for people to come into the light. A gold glowing lantern, and one big white light shows us a creative sign. We will be searching for guidance with God's help inside of the light. He just did that. The Lord will be behind us with His light. Now the Lord sends out light, and He offers a white circular glowing ball of it, holding that out behind three different people on the other side as an example, of a more giving way, and perhaps letting the glorious variations of the supernatural spirit manifest more with them. The reason the lantern which happened to turn up in the Lord's hand didn't look goofy, is because He was glorifying people inside of His spirit with a beautiful golden light, too.

The back of our Lord is uplifting three levels inside of the spirit now. His shoulders and soul which is of considerable height has a very fine outline to His robe, and for His entire self, actually. It is if He were looking over His right shoulder as He climbed higher into the light. It is getting quite interesting. Suddenly a pure white Easter basket appears, and the contents inside was a yellow bunny rabbit with dark eyes. The children inside of the heavens above have a marvelous time hunting for small and larger colored eggs.

A girl with an unusual suede bonnet upon her head, decorated with a silky and rich purple bow, holds up a soft saffron, and brighter golden egg of different proportions. Her dress is very white layered and has an assortment of printed on very small and much whiter angels. Their wings are very much spread apart, beautifully, much like the butterflies. But still an important time for people on earth to celebrate Christ. Also colorful images of angels, in assortments of yellow and white, golden white, pure gold, blue, with red and pink wings, do change in color, where children enjoy watching the beauties cling to them. They'll also bring a sense of understanding through the Lord. And should we really be that surprised, the level in which the Lord has raised our attentive state of being to was up to a place where children play?

Not by use of engines, but driven by the course of action the Lord has taken, people in heaven boating, unhurried, feel they are touring what the Lord has given them. Your family will join with you on many of the boating trips. You'll feel that you've never lost track time with them.

The out of body prophecy never ends for the interpreter, it's just second nature to see on both sides of life, day after day. A lot of times people out in public don't want to hear about it, but mostly those who do receive the most benefits, surprisingly are the brightest individuals, who truly understand. This wasn't going to be said about what the Lord just revealed, but He insists, and when the Lord wants His message heard, better just come out with it. Very black and thick enlarged clouds were pulled back and upward into the Lord's hands. He curled them back and away from us. While removing the darkness from our lives, He ever so reminds us to keep our heads up and pray into the light. Hands were folded and the golden light shines, directly after the clouds were removed. His right hand squeezed all of the clouds together, tighter and tighter, as though he wasn't ever going to give up. The Lord rubs His hands together.

A gold string harp was carefully looked at up close, which was being held in the Lord's hands now. The u-shape harp was sat down next to two more of the same, but there were still more. A very large curving harp made from gold sat with the three. The Lord, inside of this very mellow golden light, cups His right hand closely to His ear. He pressed both of His smooth hands together and rests them next to His right cheek. When we go to sleep at night is especially when Jesus and God would like to hear from us. Oh, if you knew how lucky you are.

Six perfect shape ivory buckets are very huge. They may be huge teacups you can ride inside of. Just wait a minute. Someone is trying to say that people fly with them. Expressed so enthusiastically there is no doubt. In very in depth perception of men and women, they fly around the heavens in these things, you almost have to shake your head in disbelief. But up close is where a dishwater blonde inside of one of the rides, and a young boy around ten or eleven years of age have slowed down their flying shells of an ivory cup. They don't have any handles on the outside, but they do fly freely. The two cup drivers do have an instrument panel. They took off in a hurry and must have made a full circle, because they stopped on a dime next to each other, and what a look on their face. It would be the same look in your eyes if you came to a screeching halt at the edge of a cliff. But they were safe. Gleaming tinted light of gold surrounds their beautiful ivory buckets which favor deep cups. These two people are way too cool not to keep an eye on.

Her gestures suggest that it is very desirable for us to be there with them in heaven. We wish we were. But it is true, we are there with them now. Credit has been given to us also. That may be hard to explain. She knows what you are studying with written knowledge pertaining to the information being sent mentally, spiritually, and more intuitively back and forth from their realm to ours. The blonde driver is showing off the large lit rim surrounding her flyable ride, that's overelaborate with sparkling gold lights. The boy's ride is sparkling silver glitter upon the outer rim of the gigantic cup. A white light glows in the silver glitter. Instantly arched ivory shields raise up from the back of each cup. One would perceive them as backrests. Or perhaps large ivory auras for protection. If they are them, the aura should be placed over their heads, you'd think. Inside of the holy light they are real. Back to our guests. Orange and blue streaks of color became known. Now the backside of the large cups with those strange shields of light are going away on a long path. As the flyers leave, twirling white light, identical to heavy exhaust, pours out from the bottom of the shields. It's great up here in the spirit.

We need to learn more about heaven. One thing is the Lord is obsessed with light of all color. The Lord is building a gold brick wall that extends thus near and far, but the structure surprisingly bends to make a well-rounded corner, and He continues growing it to make a point. Upon the gigantic wall there are holy white angels. Each angel has a golden halo. Nice and bright they are. Part of the wall crumbles at the corner until a full circle of white light appears. Prayer hands again. They are visible. If the Lord crumbles the enclosure, we look at ourselves within, do not sit and stew over your problems, pray to Him for relief. One of the small girly angels reached her hand out, palm side up. Her mouth was puckered, which meant she was blowing a kiss. The burst of light before her was transcendent, and the kiss was traveling gracefully through the spirit.

The long but arched edge, only, of an angelic presence lifts upward and a twinkling bronze and gold sparkle delights. A not so bright golden heart appears with the word "love" inside. But the first letter was actually capitalized. The kids are going nuts on the golden railed slides that become conjoined to moving whiteness. You can see their hands sliding down the rails as they move along swiftly behind one another. They are cute too. And they are dressed up wearing black pirate hats and Indian feathers so far. A young girl with golden pigtails just stuck her tongue out. And for fun she places three wide open fingers in front of her face so she can look between the spaces. She has a glowing yellow round button. Next she pressed that to stop the slide. You'd think she'd point that out first, before making a couple of silly faces. A very brilliant glassy golden light shined above her now. She looks over her shoulder to see if everyone is safe and ready to move along with her. But you can't see anyone behind her on the slide, although the youngster in heaven is waving, like many of the kids will do when you visit.

They're either visiting with you in the heavens as spiritual travelers, while greeting you and your friends with a friendly wave, or they'll be departing inside of the spirit. A slanting "J" comes in close, but that's not a letter, that's someone's nose. However, he or she has taken four steps backwards. Still very much a greetings of some sort from God. After visualizing two very clean white gloves, soon thereafter the person wearing them has finally rested both hands on the keyboard of a baby grand piano. Very funny so far. The gloves have moved up into the air, and the pianist has signaled the "ok" sign, as the index of the right finger and thumb joining in a circular shape. Nonchalantly the gloved hands sway gently back and forth across the keys, suggesting a very enlightening musical piece is being performed. You'd be surprised who it is. A small boy covered in white light is playing. He is no older than four or five. That is wonderful. The top of his head and flickering golden light causes a stir. He is bowing after his performance, but the light was unexpectedly, equally as stunning. A baby blue halo has arched above the boy's head now. He walks quickly with all the confidence in the world with a spring in his step.

If you care a lot for the color green, they have beautiful valleys with hills that will never cease to amaze you. To capture the everlasting landscape and the beauty, especially if you have an interest in photography, you will have any size camera that you wish for. Sworn on a stack of bibles, people inside of the Lord's kingdom are really standing in place examining pictures that they took of locations they visit. You'd think, why do they do that? We can photograph anything and see the picture, even bigger than an ordinary camera would deliver. If you are single in heaven it will be arranged for you to be with someone, and you don't have to believe this, but there is an option of resting, close by his or her side. Invitations are often accepted and you'll be able to first offer warm greetings in the privacy of your own setting.

You'll enjoy your freedom, it's given unto you abundantly. There's a man with a long nose playing a shiny banjo. His fingers are moving, where there is a good chance he is trying to teach us that all musical instruments will be played and listened to. He is also trying to tell us that it is fun playing the banjo. You'll be a good teacher, yourself. And for all of us, try not to be so stubborn and listen to the interpretations. Don't worry about a thing, the Lord is assuring that He will provide us with the best transportation inside of heaven, in a very special way to fit our needs. You will also be selecting your very own method of commuting.

We will always be pleased with the Lord's plans for us on the other side of life. You'll make wise choices when choosing what to do. There is also a particular agenda to think about. The Lord is informing the interpreter that if you have a special flower or flower arrangement in mind that you'd really enjoy very much giving to your mother and father, or grandparents, as you walk up to them in heaven, upon your arrival, just let Him know about the kind you think they'd enjoy. Especially if you presented the flowers to your loved ones in the past, which were so memorable to them, perhaps they were picked somewhere on your way home from school. That was too good to be true. The Lord held up His index finger, right up to His mouth. He will keep it a secret from them for now. A thoughtful card was shown. The Lord related that there are many miracles He can perform, and so if there were special letters or gift cards and certain items your loved ones received from you, ask Jesus in prayer to go over the sentimental value of them with you. It seems He will honor our wishes with flowers and special mementos to be offered.

After everything being said and done about the aforementioned, two bouquets of beautiful pink roses at their best, and a full group of red blossoms were nothing less than being real inside of the light. Their freshness was undeniable. Fresh water droplets made them glisten.

Now the stunning effects from a bright gold harp, that has a high back with a ball tunnel of white light resting upon its opposite end of the arch that's breathtaking. Specs of a lighter shade of gold glitter in the background on a width of more golden decor. The Lord is opening His mouth. A flow of golden light, and the presence of real water streams steadily throughout. It mixes into the water, right from the Lord's mouth it looks beautiful, the way light and water appears. Now then, down and down we go watching Him create a waterfall, upon ivory stairs, which have been glowing from the same light that overflows from His inner self. Baby lambs here and everywhere in the spirit are softer than the finest silk. The Shepherd's cane is tall and an eggshell white. With all of the ups and downs that occur, we should depend on the Lord.

People are acting out in the spirit with telephones. But in heaven they want you to call upon them, when contacting a relative through prayer, visualize them as if you were talking over the phone with them. If you listen closely, they'll whisper to you. Nothing is put on hold up above. The spirit is showing they will stop and go over important points of conversation. Leaders in paradise will instruct us on important events to come.

They think the remedy for curing cancer is down the road, and the spirit world shines its golden light in an immense way while pondering that. There are many conversations with God that go unnoticed, but that's all about to change. Before the Lord describes the whirling white light ride in heaven, He will continue relaying messages through His interpreter. Many moons ago a traveling preacher who ministered to the interpreter on the gifts of the holy spirit, communicated with him, God was about to heal his eyes. Since then the visions and out of body experiences are non-stop. And the spiritual dreams are colossal. That is how this mini-journey into heaven is happening, inside the mind of another, and through God's heavenly eyes.

It can't wait. Since the interpreter has taken the whirling white light ride in heaven, he can no longer hold his tongue. Talk about a spiritual awakening! The spirit became so vibrant and intense one evening, even though it came through a deep slumber state, there was no way on God's green earth that anyone could say the heavenly experience wasn't of the Lord's and God's doings. The light of God rolled upward with a ton of fun-loving movement. The light was very clear beneath the puffy cumulus. Up and up we go. But all of the love is up in the heavens. We know it comes from the Lord. Why such a good feeling? It feels like when you were five or six, and on the best day you have felt so good. No, even better than that.

A combination of the coolest rides ever, your mind isn't in a fog, you'll find that you have become one with God. You feel like God. You'll feel God, closely. Will the ride occur with you? Count on it. The whirling white light ride is massive in size. Ask the Lord in prayer to take you for a spin, however, the whirling part lifts you into a higher and brighter world beyond measure. You won't feel dizzy at all. And you thought that one day you would outshine the rest of us here down on earth, because you went to heaven, and saw Jesus in the light. This ride may not be new to the Lord, but it certainly was for the interpreter. If there was any way to travel to heaven in the highway of your mind, that you prefer, make that request known to the Lord. People have seen the light with out of body experiences since the stone ages. Stunning, very much indeed. But the Lord can increase the greatness you feel inside, from wanting to take a ride to heaven inside of the whirling light. You won't need a ticket to board. The Lord invites you by a simple request. Later you will be dying to leave this world. Let's receive prophecy from the Lord about what has been disclosed. The spirit is ready to communicate live, whether through visions or visible wording that often appears. The ride had to be described, but the Lord was responsible.

A bed appears with a white pillow placed at the head of it. Folded hands can be seen. The facts about the ride was truthful, that's why the Lord is coming through the light right now. The words, "Ask Me" appeared inside of the holy spirit. Just as is. A white tunnel of light sends a straight path to the bed. Not that odd since the Lord understands the situation enough to share His wisdom with us. When in bed at night, first pray to the Lord for the whirling white light ride in heaven to begin. He desires that we picture the white tunnel of light in the distance, shedding light down upon us while in bed. You can actually see it happening inside the center of darkness, deep within your spirit is where everything originates, inside of the light. Keep your eyes closed, you'll still be picturing the light coming for you, since your prayer was heard in earnest, the Lord will fulfill your heart's desire. You won't be able to stop the ride once it brings you up higher and higher into the Lord's kingdom. The fun part is the ride. White clouds will whirl on each side of your entire body, while what there is to feel is lightness and joy in your heart. It's possible your feelings will vary in comparison to others who fancy it differently.

All materialistic items and money won't even cross your mind. God will have you thinking otherwise. If your ride to heaven doesn't come soon enough for you it doesn't mean your prayer hasn't been heard. The Lord just might be assisting others right now. Keep on praying. After you have taken your "last" trip to heaven, after you are dead, gone and buried, you'll be celebrating life again. The interpreter got a little carried away, the Lord has much more to announce.

Did you know the people in heaven are cheering for you at this very moment? It's so true. Family members are the first in line. They instill confidence within. Just ask in thoughtful prayer to hear them cheer you on. You never know, in your sleep they may come and let loose on you. Don't worry about them frightening you because you'll be near them up in heaven when they come. And don't be too concerned if you don't see anyone and only hear their voice. Everyone comes well-organized in the Lord's kingdom upon His request to entertain you. If you don't happen to hear the saintly spiritual people in heaven cheering for you, even after a long period of time, just meditate on the idea of your loved ones cheering. You'll be the lucky one if you also hear hand clapping. People in heaven do have a much higher regard for life, and for you.

A super large black artist's brush is floating by inside of the spirit. If you think that's crazy, you're not the only one. If you could only see Jesus smiling. A sparkle of gold glitters nearer to His right eye. He will help. With a man and a woman sitting at paint easels, where a tremendously soft white light has manifested, they wear dark hats and light weight grey robes. The man turns his painting to reveal a golden pear, done so well you'd believe he was a true master of the arts. The lady turned her painting around quickly, almost as if she were in competition with him. Such a beautiful golden apple with a small, bright green leaf, that should surely take first prize for color and originality. They didn't come to heaven to horse around, they're enjoying the full benefits of an everlasting life. It is a bit odd, but it's to help us know what people can do.

There is skill involved, and a little magic. At a wink of an eye you'll find yourself at an easel. Many awards will be handed out, some in scrolls with tied on ribbons, and others will shine in silver and gold. A fireman in the light with his black helmet on is going to act out a scene. He is very privileged to keep his helmet. He mentioned how scary and terrible it was to have to go through flames and smoke, whereas it was very difficult for him to see, where he really had to watch his step. He is holding a babe in his arms. Quite amazing he can show us what he went through, and be here on our side of life, and on his spiritual level at the same time, visually. He knew in his heart it was all worth it to bring families out alive. There is a huge mound of heavy rock and rubble near the fireman. Only the fire helmet appears, as if it were mounted on the rock formation for a special reason. Did he die in a fire? One thing for sure is, he's praying for less tragedies, especially so that fires will cease on our side. He is saluting fellow firemen and women now. He has a golden award, and it awaits his children one day, who'll join him in heaven after they've grown up. He and his fellow firefighters will be able to share their special awards.

It is better to continue with what is known and shown. The spirit is moving up in style. The holy spirit is grateful. The Lord believes what we shall learn of, and that which we have already discovered is very beneficial. Three small golden crowns from royalty appear. Baby blue glows. Then a forth crown, much larger and glowing magnificently is the very one the Lord wears. He chooses to reveal the smaller crowns as signs relating to immense wisdom. The sequence was to gain attention. Large red, gold and soft white hearts come through.

A blue heart is a little higher up in the heavenly scheme of things. A woman is crying teardrops and uses a white handkerchief to dry them from Her face. It didn't take much time to figure out that when a jagged silver crown appeared on top of a gentlewoman's head, no other but the Virgin Mary was present. She must show you that She cares. Is this a big honor? Why, you bet! While waiting on Her to act, the crown upon Her beautiful full head of brown hair became bright. Clusters of fine diamonds began sparkling again. She cares for the lame just like Her Son does. It isn't all about the richness in Her diamonds on the lustrous crown, She really does know you're hurting inside. Why would She be shedding a tear? The word "mull" appeared. Do not over think the problems which have caused serious grief inside of your heart. She would have you know that She is holding lovely pink roses wrapped in a white wrap. You have never seen such softness in these flowers before. Mary offers Her love to the world with a beautiful rose that She now pulled from the bouquet. How is that true? She made the earth and the tunnel of white light appear at the same time. Naturally the ball of white light was on a pretty decent wide angle with the globe of earth down below. This wasn't the first time the Lord and Mary and Father God have used this illustration. She is believed to be cradling baby Jesus in Her arms. The infant wrapped in white does have brown hair. But how can Mary do that with the Christ Child, while wearing a crown on Her head? She most likely didn't own one when She walked the earth with Her child. In heaven God is powerful, and so is Mary.

Mary is like the Lord, She can do anything in the spirit. An adorable lamb is standing on all fours before Her and baby Jesus. Pretty wild but She hands over Her baby to the Godly spirit only identified at this moment, as someone with lengthy hair, mustache, and a fluffy white beard. He has been showing up inside of the spirit, off and on. Baby Jesus was in between the friendly spirit with the long flowing white robe and Herself. But in a flash, Jesus Christ, all grown up as we know Him to be, is standing front and center with His Mother and Father. Jesus wants us to be told what He thinks is right. He did lean over and kissed Mary's lovely pink cheek. You want to see a closeup of that happening? Ask in prayer, and expect the unexpected when you look up. Just a small amount of faith will help. Also, look and see if you can see one of your loved ones near them. No visions yet? Expect a miracle from above. It would help to concentrate on the light. It is an energy that surrounds you. Forgive the Lord for not being able to set things straight. It isn't a matter of a merit system when it comes to the Lord granting us special visions and out of body experiences, you need to understand His existence first.

Puffy cotton balls of white light seems to be preoccupying the mind right now. Why do they want that in heaven? Time to ask in prayer. God is observant and enjoys creating many forms out of spiritual light. The back edge of an angel's ivory wing taps the very tip of it into the spirit world, which created a blue patch of light now. On the opposite side from that angel an identical cherub backed up its own tip of the wing in the direction of its mate, and blue formed. The same two partners have a glowing yellow of light above them. The color expands over the angels and presents a new perfectly formed yellowy wing, behind the ivory wings. White robes are finally visible with long and neat creases. Around the necks of the angels were sparkling gold rings of light, that highlighted small gold crosses that they wore. They are angelical sisters of the light. And very pretty lady like angels. One of the angels folds her hands, and you should have seen them. What was so special? She made the structure of the Lord's church appear in her hands, just from folding them together with her index fingers pointing up. It is for certain she wasn't holding a picture or a model of a church. The angel's wings have spread open in the back.

They have two sets of matching wings. The female angel who enjoys praying in the name of the Lord and for the sake of His church, had rolled out a wide bundle of black satin. The cloth unfolds and unfolds, falling downward. Someone is picking up the end. And how she managed to roll down the long sheet of satin without, first, anyone taking hold of the end to pull it away from her is stranger than fiction. Then again, did her angelic friend become invisible and pull the satin away from her? Both of their glowing halos just brightened. Maybe we are getting warm. The angelic female rolling it out takes the very end up where she is and twists the satiny piece of cloth, before pressing it up to her face for feeling the softness. She related that her friend was beside her all along. That was in spirit talk. If you are smiling that's what they wanted from all of us. One of the girls has her hands on her hips. Easily told from watching them pressing against her white robe. One thing she created from the satin was a large black ribbon, the kind you would see given out for first, second and third place prize levels.

There is a special request inside of the kingdom of God to hear your prayers. You can believe this, in a two-tone somber golden light Jesus has His own hands folded in prayer. He is smiling. He needs people to trust Him. Why in the world would the Lord be appearing so often to the interpreter? Lucky! The Lord is sitting at a table. But it isn't so wide, more of a convenient setting for Him to rest His hands. Silky white angels are in a row beside Him, making heaven ever so believable as perfection. The Lord wants you to know there are settings with the saints. Two dark haired men with mustaches and beards, now are sitting on each side of the Lord. They tilted their heads more to show they're trying to understand and believe the ways of our Lord. Although they were now at the table with our Savior, it seems Jesus may have stepped out for a moment. There was only heavenly light between them. Can you believe the two guests of the Lord have turned to each other with silver crosses in their hands? They are very overwhelmed by the power in the cross is why they're at His table in the first place. Hopefully that's saying something meaningful regarding the two men. Why are there two yellow tulips in their presence? We can all agree it's better than having itch weed. And if flowers make the saints feel happy, we feel happy for them. The colorful courtyards will simply amaze you.

A woman with a dirty face and scraggly dark hair has raised her hands to the Lord in prayer. She reminds us of someone ready to dive into a pool. Apparently she studied a little bit of witchcraft while living on earth. She wasn't burned to the stake, but there is a fire burning behind her. Her black garment is badly torn, more of a rag left on her. There is hope that she uses prayer for redemption. She felt that she was bad, and even calls out to Jesus on her knees now. A small gold cross is above her in the light, and instantly the Lord raised her up to comfort the woman close to His chest, whereas, she's gazing up into the Lord's eyes with love inside of her own too. The Lord reveals the bottom of a magnificent white robe that pleases the woman, who was now turned around one hundred percent. Her face was of cleanliness, and her flushed cheeks would astonish everyone.

But the Holy Bible was shown. Does that mean that God disapproves of witchcraft? It is not the word of God. The Lord's very strong hand sets upon her left shoulder as they face forward in the light. And that's what the Lord is all about, love.

Several white rings have displaced themselves from a cloud. People of all ages from more mature adults to young children are seated on some sort of golden chair, facing sideways. After the white rings of light had fallen out the people down below began adjusting them upon the top of their heads. Ever heard of too many gifts from God? They inform not to worry about enough to learn, or for that matter, enough to do.

Days in heaven are filled with love. You will be very delighted about the way you feel about your life with the Lord in heaven. The many promises He has made will not be broken. Blue spots and a white one are evident. They are not causing dizziness, therefore, they come from the spirit. Three small keepsake boxes are lined up, almost appearing like treasure chests. A cheerful lady turns her back to the Lord while He removes a pearl necklace, from the container to place around her neck. But the necklace consists of many small ivory pearls. She was given an ivory heart, that's attached at the bottom. Beautifully printed on the front of the locket was the word, "Grace." The woman with the long brown hair down to her waistline was receiving another fine reward for being the Lord's and Father God's daughter. A gold ring upon her right hand is topped with a soft glowing ball of white light that's glittering with gold and silver. She rushes away, but turns around where you'll see her standing with a small group of female and male friends, where she is happily showing off her gifts. The holy spirit is starting to move up higher in the light, at least the Lord is demonstrating movements suggesting that He wants us to continue on with our spiritual ride in through the heavens. We 'll be focusing on the light.

The Lord wants to help. Two white crosses planted within the spiritual light, are resting on a slight tilt. They represent fallen soldiers, because there's an infantry man from the army with an old world one or world war two helmet in his hand, covering his stomach area. He wants to relay messages. First, blue light glows. He points out that he used those two large tents in the background. They looked like circus tents a little. He is trying to tell us a story. On bended knee he's kneeling before the white crosses. He was very sorry for war, and now is very clear about the war in which he and his friends were involved with. It was the first world war. A large and very perfectly formed number one appeared. His army helmet is being touched by an enormous golden sunlight. The gentleman stands back some, to where he becomes very visible, as if we were looking at someone from our side. He looks human, but the brave soul is a spirit too.

The soldiers carry themselves with pride and dignity on the other side of life. Both of his hands are buried in his face. Gradually his face lifts, but only his left brown eye is opening. The right eye isn't exactly an empty socket, it is made up of glowing white light. The soldiers do march in ceremonial parades for the people of heaven, with even revealing depictions of what had happened on the battlefields. The marching bands are never too noisy to listen to. We will see injured soldiers bandaged up from their war wounds, but in a split second, they'll be without them. They feel it is necessary to learn what war was like, for those of us who're somewhat, unknowing. Perhaps the soldier went on his way down that beautiful pathway in the light, where many soft white petaled flowers are being strewn from left to right. The thing is they come to light alright, but you can't see anyone pitching the flowers. They are of such delicate beauty.

Now there are two flower girls, one on the right side of the long pathway, and the other girl dressed in a soft flowing white robe, similar to the friendly spirit across from her with resembling brown hair. They have white flower wreaths on their heads. Soft and beautiful. Picture the Lord in giant size looking down upon the girls, respectively so. He can see how hard they are working away decorating the path for Him. They are equal in the Lord's mind as people. Both of the flower girls are side by side, with charming woven baskets, heading up the pathway.

A change was needed. The Lord's spirit is moving about to create more room for His people. You'd think there was enough already, everlastingly. That's what it becomes. We can't expect the Lord to be immediately self-satisfied. He works inside of the kingdom to improve stature. It's obvious someone was just lifted up into the light. But the Lord has twins in His arms, or two babies nearly the same age. It's a nice experience to watch Him with children. It's necessary for their well-being, repeatedly bringing small ones into the light, by way of the Lord cradling and holding them in His arms. Even though light was detected around the babies, His hands were seen beneath them as they were rising up to where the Lord wanted them to be. And you think that you won't sit front and center to watch the Lord perform such sensational acts? The sandaled left foot bends back and upward. That was after several golden flowers without their stems made the King's cross in the pattern in which it was. Naturally the flowery cross was laying flat before the Lord. Praise our holy Lord Jesus for His work.

A string of twinkling tiny gold lights are ravishing as they shine. A slanted zebra-striped halo is upon a young lad's head. He is ghostly white. He holds a white candle that's glowing softly and yellow. The lad blew out the candle, but have no fear a white flame of light replaces the yellow one. That angelic lad has a lot of flair. The boy winks and the white tip of the flame sparkles with a small arch of gold glitter that remains above the light.

The spirit is moving. First comes one child, then two and many more in a choir. What's unusual is they're in heaven with their little hymn books in hand. The spirit prints out the word, "listen." Do you hear anything? As an adult female brunette steps forward with a very long white robe on, covering her from neck to toe, it's obvious that she is very tall. She begins to sing with the children. It wouldn't be so unusual, but when spirits keep congregating on their side, and not on ours, they're beginning to raise some eyebrows. A huge gold horseshoe is shining, and it is valuable to the Lord, as a symbol, Him wishing the people in the world luck and good fortune. Are there not signs and wonders coming to you, especially when you sleep at night?

Begin to experience the hereafter by becoming more intuitive, firstly. Once that happens, you'll be in heaven before five o'clock dinner is ready, and back in time to enjoy a healthy meal. Sitting and breathing here and in heaven is a synch. Ask in prayer to see the light. Look up, remain silent and very still. Using your eyes look from left to right. Something is moving around. Not in your mind, alone, but inside of the room. Don't fret it could be a relative on the other side of life coming in. Small intervals of smooth white light might appear. Or there could be constant formations from the eternal source of light. The visions will come from God and the Lord. Why not share an idea or two on how to see into the afterlife?

Look for a sparkling gold bell. It wouldn't have been mentioned, but the Lord insisted on that. A misty white trail of light is directly behind it. There is a white angel's wing. Then there are two. Even though they're on a side angle, seek them out if you can't see the bell and the light. They are very delicate. At this time bright spots of gold and white may even appear, which means the Lord would have you become more aware of the spiritual side of life through His very own handiwork. Is there a sparkle of gold before you now? Using the awesome power of your mind, do observe freely. It is just another way to prove the Lord knows every thought you have and will formulate. Anything that comes through the light puts you straight right dab in front of your Creator. The Lord's or it was God's hands are openly cupped inside of the holy spirit, and the sight of gleaming gold light from them was immeasurably rich and powerful. A smiling face and a Lord wearing a white robe and a matching carnation above His heart was special. Do you see Him? Keep looking, He is not shy. The flower is there before your eyes. Don't turn away from the spirit, keep looking forward if you will. If the white carnation appears, Jesus is trying to come through for you to see Him. Do not be confused if you don't see the Lord appear on our side though. He is for everyone, but if it isn't your time to see Him, then so be it.

Crushed velvet black heart pillows with a small diamond upon each awaits someone coming to heaven, or for very special people already present. A very red velvety, high backed chair trimmed with golden light around the top is just one of the chairs we'll be feeling much comfortable sitting upon. You'll feel if the plan has been set in stone with the Lord and your Father. And the gold sparkling cross is present.

There's a prominent doctor in the spirit world, if not many, who is examining a person, believe it or not, on our side of life. He leans forward from inside of the light, wearing all white, along with a stethoscope set against a man's chest. The word "tension" arrived in the message, while here and inside of the doctor's spiritual realm. It was to be explained that your messages coming from the heavens should not be ignored, that when you feel that you see health related issues communicated within the spirit, bear in mind, you could be receiving a vital warning that may save your life. The doctor bows way down as he folds his hands to say a prayer. Therefore, when heavy tension begins to ruin your day, remember that even doctors pray, and the greatest spiritual physician alive is Jesus and God who will need to be called upon.

How does the holy spirit move all of these images around? It's as if He has a collage of things happening. The Lord just said, "I am preparing to greet you in the light." Let's hope it's not our time. He means well. If you can read words in the light, well done. Our Father loves everyone on earth. Two huge black and grey tornadoes appear from the Lord setting even more examples to study and ponder. Mother nature is responsible. The tunnel of white light is in a lower position, while the globe of earth is up higher. We think just the opposite, but wait and see what you'll find out from the teacher above. Smashed homes with scattered wood piles and debris and occupants who are weeping need help. What is totally likeable is the Lord's hands dip right down and are cupped, but very open and giving. His hands have not only gathered, but rest beneath the top of a crushed structure near where the chimney once was. His hands remind one of a steam shovel scooping up debris. Another home nearby turns from rubble to a newly built structure. Yes, the Lord feels we should rebuild and get on with our lives. If we join together we can make things better. A bed and a pillow comes in the light again, but it is our warning in our dream state where we'll see these active tornadoes heading our way, in real life, if we dream them.

To be spun around inside of a nasty tornado and be tossed around like a rag doll is unthinkable for most of us. But if that should happen, the whirling white light ride in heaven, while bringing you on up to heaven through the gyrating motion of it becomes more of a joyful experience. That should never happen where we enter heaven through the likes of a bad tornado causing our death. Although the goodness yet to come will be there for young and old, when we rest upon the heavenly clouds of white light shining in various shades. It is a very youthful state of mind.

Explore the spirit. A big black treasure chest in the light. Not the small variety now. Stacked to the top edge are scads of shiny gold coins and silver. A large hand closes the lid and just rests upon the lid. Kind of funny when you see just one hand, but nothing to joke about. Suddenly two large black treasure chests open with gleaming gold coins inside, while one trove has been tipped over, revealing more coins spilling into a pile in the heavens. Between the Godly spirit's two fingers, one silver coin, with a small white angel spread across the piece, becomes a showing. The word "valuable" appears in bold black letters. We would probably be inclined to think that the gold and silver would be more valuable to us on our side of life, but God believes that His angels have just as much equal value. White light shines upon the treasures and all of the coins turn white. Hands were placed behind each large chest, and let it be known, they were closed. By hands that where covered in white light. You wouldn't be able to prove His or her hands were really all white though. Because when it comes to changing in appearance, our heavenly Father's hands may become black, or perhaps seen in a far different light of color.

Jesus is whistling and He enjoys what He hears from the sound. You would have to see Him to know for sure. His lips are puckered and sure enough, that's exactly what He is doing inside of His holy spirit right now. Before He started whistling a joyful tune He created two very interesting white curvature forms at each side of the throne. He did so. The bottom to His robe was seen, besides His bent knees, while relaxing upon a throne glowing softly of whiteness. His throne does change of color within the adjustments He so desires. Jesus was standing up creating such joys of wonderment when whistling. That's right, before your very eyes, the Lord will be seated in royalty upon the mighty throne in less than a blink of an eye. And once again, He makes you wonder, how did He do that? In front of the throne now sits two silvery and gold glowing high rimmed containers of real grapes. On His left were the green bunch overflowing from its edge, and over to the right were very ripe purple grapes to ponder. And you think that only some of the Gods and human beings had grapes? We know much more than that. The Lord has very fine means of containing the colorful fruits, that's for sure.

Golden pears that have green leaves are simply positioned upright, where they have been placed on individual curled layers of white light. That's very much so in front of the Lord, but spaced apart. Pointed feathery objects that are multi-color of pink on top, white in the middle, and blue on the bottom, not very wide or tall, glow inside of the kingdom as though they are hanging in mid-air. There are no strings attached. Everything in the heavens are smooth and cool.

Don't worry you won't need to worry about being hurt over in the spirit land of light. This is too good to be true, especially for the single man very much interested in lovely females. On the other side of life three very buxom women are greeting many travelers of the light, who're also light workers of the universe and of heaven. Sweeping back and away from the top of their heads are white see-through veils and these well-figured women have the loveliest lengthy tresses. White light just continues to discharge from the back of them. They look like harem girls.

And all women who enter the light, when it becomes their time, will also see major changes in the way their top area looks. One of the ladies with dark hair raises both of arms up as high as possible, and when she brings them both downward, she is worshiping the Lord on her knees now. What's up with the other two ladies? Why weren't they bowing down before their Master? But like small children now all three of them are sitting, with two of them on the Lord's left side, with the other woman in front of Him. Jesus sits way far back in the distance, yet very visible still to discern exactly what is happening with the four. Suddenly very closeup in the spirit, one of the women stands up and starts dancing. Around her waistline many of the golden flashes of light are helping her enjoy the dance, and to compliment the way she feels about her Lord. Her fingers were rubbing together to bring forth golden flickers of light from the tips.

The day may have changed down here on earth, but these out of body experiences never end, especially when the gift involves seeing in the light, and here on the physical level at the same time. Are the blind being shunned by the Lord? Not at all. They have special gifts waiting for them. They'll often cause people in heaven to stop and congratulate them over their newly restored gift of eyesight, while friends and family will be ready to see those who they love, healed in the very beginning. Slowly the blind will adjust with perfect eyesight in heaven.

For being on this side of life there sure is a lot of small white, surrounding clouds of light. And close by it is either the Lord's, Father God's or Mary's gold throne. But it is miniature in size. Small clouds made from light everywhere and a throne seems unoccupied. Never for a second, but they do have important errands to run. Viewing everything is indeed very heavenly. They let you feel in charge of the their throne room a little. How sweet it is. All in all if Jesus wanted to let loose and give us everything He has in eternity, we'd be viewing His and at least Father God's throne on bended knee with a much different viewpoint.

Funny how the holy spirit's movement appeases us. Different from dark angel's wings, three ship's sails are cast set to sail, somewhere on the cabalistic shores of heaven. Instantly bright, but very clear, white light reveals a very good view of what the ships look like. They are not gigantic, but not very small either. They rest upon calm and clear water. Each ship carries the holy symbol of a white cross in the center of its bulging sail. A very young boy squatting at the edge of the water is now playing with a small boat of his own. He wears a pair of tan shorts and a pale orange, short sleeve shirt. Viewing the three sail boats with a changing view of them, they've sailed on out to distant shores in the light, unless they have just been greatly minimized.

Far away they are small. Strangely the boy's reflection in the water is quite amazing to see himself, closer than within the first familiarization of the child in heaven. He has a full head of brown hair, and he couldn't be past the age of six or seven. He enjoys tinkering with his toy. He moves the small toy boat with the white sail when he feels the strong urge to make it go. All he has to do is think of the boat going and it sails. His intuitive side is very magical. Floating green lily pads attached to purple flowers are beautiful in the water as they reach the shoreline where the boy is standing up while enjoying such a radiating orange light, that's enough to make you want to give up your Sunday afternoon for. The child isn't tired of playing with his toy, but he holds it close to himself now, before lifting it up to rest upon a white pedestal, close to where many white flowers are hanging loosely from limp vines. He takes a flower and touches a round ball of white light with the petals. The whole white flower turns as big as the ball of light, and the light behind it flows inside, around, and throughout it entirely so.

Obstacles are being removed one after another with the white eternal light, brightening more and more. A super big black sword, and a black shield that carries the symbol of a white cross is visible here inside of the light. This time a heavily armored soldier in black is lifting his helmet from his head with a bowed head. An example from the Lord of the times that came before us. But every knee shall bow before the Lord. Pure soft yellow light shines upon the soldier as he worships our Lord on bended knee. In between the planet earth and the everlasting tunnel of white light is a white cross. But if we are inside of heaven receiving great spiritual messages, how could it be true that our planet and the more advanced way of life in the hereafter has escaped us? It never will be far from our reach, unbelievable, spiritual substantiation is more to our greater benefit when we believe the Lord has good intention still.

Premeditation is a wonderful attribute to Him. Feel as if you are out in space, in a way, it's only your mind appreciating visions. The spiritual Lord of ours is presenting a large white envelope. Affixed on the front is a red stamp. In bold black lettering, "Father God." Even though just a hand held open against an ear came in view, what the Lord and Father God wants His people to hear is that, we are very precious to them. Communicate any way possible. The interpreter just heard the word, "easy." And while observing the fine spiritual aspects of heaven and its habitants, that word also had appeared.

A young man likely to be around twenty years of age with blonde bangs is peeking over the edge of a top hat. Quite innocent indeed. A very cute cinnamon color to rabbit's ears pop up, and out from the hat. The rabbit's eyes are very dark, but shiny too. The hat has tilted forward, whereas on the inside, the most adorable sight of mixed colored baby bunnies brings a warmer smile. They fit inside of the hat as snug as a bug. And is this spiritual young man inside of the light a trained magician? The top hat has enlarged itself, magically, so he just may be trained in magic after all. The magician has a small baby duckling resting in the palm of his hand now. His hand lowers and lowers, and he finally rests the chic next to many grown ducks who have much glistening silver light over their resting area. Behind each duck and all baby chicks, by just looking at them up close, their glowing yellow, angelic shaped wings of light is a guide of sorts.

The young magician is back. Now not only does his face appear, he visits wearing a buttoned down white coat, which has small shiny silver buttons. He is performing for us. His right hand nearly reaches his ankle with a spinning yellow top upon the flat side of his hand. He reaches out with his left hand, between two very white clouds, one that is a little smaller than the other. But as he continues spinning the top around down below, it starts turning more gold around the middle, until all you see is that and silver and white stars decorating it. He smiles inside of a mild golden light now. He whirled the clouds into a spinning top. Did he wrap the two clouds around the top by using the power of his mind during the spinning process? Beautiful streaks of violet light provides a little pleasure. Now everything has changed in the magician's act. He examines both of the spinning tops at eye level. These tops are pretty big. They have both been turned to gold with black swirls from a skillful mind and resourcefulness. There are glittering silver and white stars of all sizes that topped them off as well.

You know there is a very divine visitor inside of the Lord's kingdom, who came as quite shocking, to say the least. He was dressed in a floor length white robe, but what was more unusual was the glowing bead necklace of many colors that was worn around His neck. Some of the colors were white, pink, blue, yellow and purple, along with orange. What kind of man spirit wears a necklace that could even glow in the dark? First, let the world know He is the warmest, kindness, and most gentlemanly spirit the heavens have given unto us. By looking at His face alone, you'll become a little weak in the knees. Yes He did have shoulder length long brown hair, a mustache and a beard in His features. Something in His face wasn't all that human, nor was it difficult to understand what He was conveying inside of the penetrated spiritual light.

If we were to count second by second, we'd see that this kind spirit's face had many more features than a normal human being. Not to sound cruel, He held wonderful animalistic features, but they were not fierce, only gentle in spirit. We'll most likely meet up with Him again in heaven. How could He present Himself in every nationality at the same time too? Well, He did and that's that. Only mere seconds went by seeing all of these extraordinary features. When we are in heaven God will show us how He has become Asian, Hebrew, Jewish, Swedish, German, Caucasian, African, Italian, French, Polish, Swedish, and never to forget, most importantly, every nationality and God given creature, whom He has ever created. Wait until you see Him. Perhaps the interpreter is taking the situation in his own hands, believing in a God who is to believed to have visited him inside of the holy spirit, and is urging others, to at least to try understanding that the spiritual leader in the light has come to help all that He can in the universe. What if it was the Lord who brought such a clear understanding in this manner? Would He be the same as God?

Some might think that. Although some would not, because, supposedly they would tend to believe the Lord couldn't pay you a visit, but they would really not know at all. While pondering the out of body tour into the light, the same spiritual entity has arrived. He would like us not to forget that He carries a gold cross above His heart, that is being worn at the moment. Interestingly the yellow glowing bead to the necklace upon His neck has cast light upon His cross. His hands lower, and they have opened up. Inside of each hand is a small gold cross. A sky blue color flashes, and the holy spirit moves in such a jovial motion, it has been detected our spiritual guest of honor is full of love, laughter and happiness.

To say and to tell you what is seen inside of the light. An Asian lady wearing a huge straw hat with a chin strap is presently gathering important information in the light, and is beginning to share with us what she feels is right. One thing for sure, this lady has a lot of soul and purpose in her life. She has some fresh daisies inside of her hand and sits them down at a gravestone. The name, "Mother" is engraved on the grey stone. There seems to be a fitting and most honorable gesture about placing flowers and visiting deceased loved ones who've passed on. How original is that to do such a thing, though, because her mom would have to be with her in the light, if that were the case with the special visitation now? A tall and slender yellow gleaming light pole with a shedding white light on top is enough evidence of both, her and the mother remaining inside of the light, where these messages and visions have started from. The ladies are quite beyond the norm. Both with shoulder length shiny black hair, and a youthful appearance to die for, there's a glowing golden light which blends in with their brown eyes. The daughter is watering spring daisies in heaven, using an ideal watering can. It isn't silver, but quite tan with a convenient loop for a handle. At least we know that we'll be able to water our own personal flower gardens. You may tend to flowers as much as you like. There is something you should know.

The interpreter had experienced an out of body experience, once, in a dream state, that's just as noteworthy. A spiritual man wearing a long white robe, and a very colorful glowing beaded necklace around His neck, walked up to him just for a casual visit. But with six other people in the spirit, sitting casually across the way, listening attentively to the interpreter complain that he may have a little bit of cancer inside of his body. One of them commented clearly on that. And keep in mind, everyone was inside of the holy spirit on the other side of life, out of their body and into the spirit world of knowledge. The wise man across from the interpreter, and the spiritual man with the glowing beads, had said back in regards to the cancer concern, "It can be overridden." In other words, we can overcome, or prevail over our concerns regarding serious cancer illnesses. They know better than we what can be cured, using a little bit of faith and mind over matter. That is truly one message from the light we won't be calling, "weird."

Gentle is the holy spirit, in a peaceful way they show love from above. They want you to know they are ready to pick you up when you fall. Preferably, we shall remain strong. Small houses can be seen down below on the earthly surface, just to give you an idea how far up inside of the light the holy spirit has brought the interpreter, yet with feet planted firmly on the ground, this is just another good example of how mysterious the Lord works. With fireplaces burning wood aglow, hot flames bring warmth amongst God's people. The earth appears from the Lord again, and the word "created" in dark lettering comes, too. A man who is bare chested working outdoors in the heat bends over as he wipes sweat off the side of his head with the edge of his hand. The wording "Given Unto Man" appeared. To the Lord and God Almighty that would be proper English. And they could have said that in any given language. No, English is not favored over all other languages, in fact the Lord and His Father speak all languages fluently, whether you be with them in heaven, or on earth, they'll communicate with you through the holy spirit in your language any day of the week. So the world has been given unto man to work the soil and harvest food on his own. But God and His Son will be guiding us on a spiritual mission today, one many non-believers would be frightened to even listen to, or for that matter, believe that they're able to go on and enjoy it with the rest of us. Praise the Lord and pass the ammo, but please do not kill the messenger. The Lord is ready to sit you upon the mountain top of glory. He has attempted to reveal two tall mountains with very nice and generous amounts of glowing purple light, which outclass any of the countless numbers of mountainous regions that have been created.

Many silver and gold crystals of light drift by in the light, that which has been created will never be destroyed. They'll be passed by on occasions, but will be remembered from the glorious beauty it represents. There is a game that you'll think that is most interesting. A man on the right facing a woman in a somber golden light that's covering them, are concentrating on each other's thoughts, by applying slight pressure to their temples with their hands against their own face. They think about what is going on through the other person's thoughts. They pick up on the other person's thoughts, intuitively. Yes they'll talk back and forth in heaven, but this is a special game that they want to clue us in on before we meet other people like them. They can also make each other feel comfortable by sending messages telling them that they'll be fine.

The woman holds up a very clean piece of paper, but in light form, and then points down below to where a man is sitting, covered in all white light, he has an even brighter halo above his head. But a widening white light from the heavens spreads outward, and down upon him, enabling the man to feel much peace of mind, the way it was meant for him to feel. We can send well-wishes to the ailing, and even use the light source from above. Use the powers of your mind. Picture your friends with a clean white halo over their head. Our friends in the light also know what's going on by perfect sight of images behind their friends, who they play the concentration game with. The Lord will give clues or the answers that they seek out. If it is demonstrated inside of the light it has to be fun. Many people on our side already know how to converge on the spiritual light. There's a white line of light. Above it is angelic person growing on that side of life. Below the level of light, where the man rests, another white angel appears, but there doesn't seem to be a face associated with the existence, only a ball of bright white light for the head and arched wings. The angel still is pretty. We would all be proud to own the little darling. The man within his very own white light on earth deserves to have all of the attention. He may be sick.

For you a spiraling pale yellow candle with a bright orange flame is in sight, closeup. Picture a spiral staircase. You can almost see through the candle, basically. But the inner part had shades of darkness. The Lord has lit His light in order to bring us through the darkness, so it seems. Pure blueness in the background enlightens. However, only some came through the light. You just want to dive through the light to get more of that feeling of beauty from the other side. This is nice. In a distance people from many walks of life and of many ages are flying downhill inside of long whirls of white light. You can see many rows of people spread apart, cheering, while some are making even funnier expressions, not unfamiliar to us, but in more of an enlivened feeling. That ride is enough to cash in all of your chips over. To give an example, hopefully to be a good one, if you have a sense of humor you'll understand. The ride looks like a super giant white caterpillar with people's faces seen above the light, which is whirling, and gliding through heaven. Do go ahead and question the ride. That's not the only surprise they have in store.

People in the spirit world will be relaying messages to everyone from the upper throne room, where the Lord, Mary, and Father God rest in glory. They'll be random messages, very spiritual in nature when least expected. Not only while you're here on earth, but when you've arrived in heaven and are going about your merry way. It is of a delicate nature, there in the spirit. Overall, you'll be very grateful for the ongoing learning experience. The true essence of spirituality will be captured in heaven. The misdeeds and mistakes known of while you were on earth will all be forgiven. Picture that big eraser still working away in the back of your mind, ridding oneself of what we have felt very guilty over in the past. Just erase away your heartaches, because you know that's what God's intentions were all along. Time to chalk one up, instead of living with self-blame and persecution. You know Jesus, He would like us to clean the slate once and for all.

Do you see that pink soft light before you? You could if you look for the light. Just by knowing the spiritual God light is all around you, any vibration in color will be presented. Sometimes the varied color of light is to soothe your tired nerves. A nice looking pink angel wing about four feet tall appeared with a glowing gold ball of light at the bottom of its wing. Why only one wing and no halo? After a short prayer asking the Lord, exquisite gold glittered on the fringe of the wing from top to bottom. But what sort of prophecy is that? A good enough of one if you can capture the beauty within your mind. A small white flocked tree displaying a pure white star upon the top is similar to a Christmas tree in the spirit. Suddenly, not one, nor two or three golden angels wings spread out between the many branches, but so many of them do, they have turned the entire tree into gold sparkling lights. The star on top even turned gold, and you can bet on it having a glorious gold cross in the center now, unlike with the full white star.

Another flocked tree is here in the holy spirit. Just simply very beautiful, more so on account of each branch securing a red cross, sticking up high so the people in the spirit know why they have been placed there. Give to people who are in need. But we are to benefit from the sighting, since we are God's helpers doing a little bit of His work, charitably. Visibly a gold cross was already in place at the point of the tree on top. Two white gift boxes with thin black ribbon tied into a bow sat on a forty five degree angle inside of a vision. From the very wrapping on one of the gift boxes below, gold light shines out and upward. Even the Lord is giving thought to what He shows. But we already know that He is remindful of a precious gift, He has given unto all of us living, and who will be in the future, an eternal life in His idea of a respectable existence.

Pure water is trickling over numerous small egg shaped stones, tan in color, leading from one level to the next downward. While seeing a solid staircase created from the stones it appears between the gradual waterfall, coming more into view it has become known that the water does not lay dormant on the steps, thus it's leading to a place in heaven, right where a flat surfaced area of white light glows where many different size rocks and boulders sit in a large waterway.

We very well understand that this is a study from beyond, and it's turning out to be quite beautiful inside of our inner most thoughts. The water can be seen very closeup in the spirit, where the Lord is changing it, now from full waves of sparkling silver water, to steady streams of golden glittery waters. Intense water is spraying upward from several spots. They are comparable to many sprinklers being set off all at once. The watery scenery is much more clear to where the spraying jets gushing up from beneath the golden surface of the waterway is almost white, apparently from the holy light surrounding the surface. Strange movement provides a v-shape full width of solid gold light to lift up, and incredibly it glows upon the fresher springs.

But people are on bended knee in their smooth white robes near the water. They are praying, giving thanks for a fresh start in life. The words "Oh Lord" came from one man's mouth as he was up on his feet now with a very sincere and fixed gaze upon his face, meant mostly for the Lord. The wording was even gold in color and well deciphered. The Lord's white sleeves and caring hands reach forward again, touching this man who is standing near the water.

The more mature child of God begins praying again, and we shall believe it is for those who are still ill on our side. A gold decorative pattern of really small flowers appear near the bottom of the Lord's robe. A long stem white flower bends downward while laying upon our Lord's lap, and it's more apparent it hasn't shriveled up. There is a vibrant green leaf attached. The flower flips over the Lord's left leg. Looking at Him, another flower of the same kind just lays upon His right knee. More of the Lord's knees up to His waistline is visible. A soft amber light is causing a warm glow all over His lap. It is kind of a special gift to see inside of the light, just like you are beginning to think, even more than before. A black bow unravels width wise, and when it reaches its end, slightly limp, though, at the opposite side, where the decorative item began loosening a sparkling gold light was shining, thereafter.

The Lord will continue to be of assistance. You don't really know if He said that or if it just came from the interpreter's mouth. Everlasting life changes everything. There are more than just a few delegates serving the Lord who'll be ready in heaven to help you begin to feel more comfortable inside of a more religious and spiritual setting. They will not damn you, only to assist in your decisions. They'll distant themselves from you, too, especially at first they tend to hang back a little, standing at high podiums. Beautiful light surrounds them. Mostly as an intended guide. You won't be badgered. You'll always feel bliss though. A nice area to walk in through and by as you go on your way is a holy temple coming into view, where the many gold crosses glow and sparkle. But a huge gold cross has a God given holy vibration about it in the presence of the other crosses beneath it, where an assembly of angelic children stand behind each of them. Magically the children's gowns turn into sparkles of gold, while the crosses turn all white. In a split second all of the children appeared to be sitting, facing the huge gold cross up above. They've reached a more comfortable level, more orderly. A violinist's violin has turned a mild yellow in color. Someone has a bow resting upon the strings. The children are very visible. They are standing up inside of Christ's temple, cheerfully clapping their small hands together. One boy is whistling. A little gold spark of light came from his hands. The children inside of heaven are very convincing and quite comical.

The spirit of the Lord is leading us into the desired direction of our Majesty. It is His honored privilege. The Lord is trying to relate where to begin with knowledge attained from Him on the other side. He isn't kidding around either. There are a few feathery ostriches prancing around, funny to look at, well worth the smile they'll put on your face up there. All possibilities exist. No death for these fine creatures just everlasting life. Very interesting how we shift from one very holy temple of God to a petting zoo. What the heck, God's temple is just about everywhere in heaven. There are two of the extremely long neck ostriches sniffing around down low, bobbing their small heads around, while really eyeballing each other back and forth. That's because they know what's happening between man and woman in the physical world, besides knowing more than we think they do in their sweet spiritual level where they are. The changes are swift.

It has been well informed that there well be gala events in your honor. Our own personal name will be sung. The music will be included, where you'll either hear the Lord, or Mary and God singing to you and your family, otherwise, choirs will sing in honor of everyone present, and naturally everyone will be able to sing all at once. There are special lyrics made about you and your feelings, and especially the Lord has them stored inside of His heart for you, ready to be sung. You'll understand why He loves you so much. A bit of a young lady stands near the Lord's side. She has very light brown long hair, and with white light about, it's easy to tell Jesus is describing to her about when she was just a little baby, which He shows with them, that the image of the child was of her when born. The words "Bless

You My Dear" appear in black lettering. A very long string of pearls hang down from her neck, only because of receiving them from her Savior. They were as clear as day. One golden streaking light shoots down from the high heavens and reaches the location where the Lord and His daughter were. Three more streaks, or rays of narrow golden light, concurrently, have now reached them from behind.

The Lord is a deep thinker. He turns to His left and studies a golden u-shape harp before His eyes. Gently He rests His right hand across the harp's strings, ready to play. Three of His fingers are straight, but His index finger curls around a single string. To be believed, but if you do not, that's alright with the Lord. He manages to present Himself from behind the harp, although He doesn't rise above it, the Lord is seeing through the harp with His face visibly behind the strings. What a pleasant soft gold light upon His face, aglow. Picture the harp appearing before you, and you'll see Him playing it now, and the Lord is still watching from the other side. But your eyes must be lifted, not once, not twice, but perhaps three or more times upward.

The bluest blue ever appeared. Between the light a straight line of whirling white light in sections continue to move forward. You have to laugh. A boy covered in a hint of yellow light is riding inside of the one whirling white light. While squinting a wee bit to try and understand him better, the boy actually holds a megaphone up to his mouth. He is making an important announcement. It's so very true, and here we go. The words inside of the holy spirit which appeared near the boy, says, "All Aboard Now." An orange and gold spark of eternal light, mixed in as one color glitters very near the child inside of his ride that he finds fun and real exciting. The adventure in heaven, the boy finds more to be than just imaginative, and the whirling white light ride is just as quick as a monorail, knowing from the in depth perception of his journey. The lad is so confident in himself, you can see him waving goodbye with a flat hand held high.

But we can pickup more awareness in the spirit now, as the way is bright clear to trek onward. The edge of a rocky mine is in sight with a white light not only shining in through the opening, from a man's helmet, but his light bounces off the rocks and glows beneath his feet as well. As though the walls of rock mirrored it, and even though that has taken place, somehow the large rocks had a divined reflection of clarity afterwards. The man is studying rock formation. And another thing, he is dressed like a scientist in a long white coat. First a large uncut green emerald, and then a vibrant red ruby surfaces. Now he has another emerald before him, but that one is cut to perfection in its own right. He has now stumbled across many small diamonds that he shows in the palm of his hand. A man wearing a jeweler's mask, sitting at a table comes to light. The global visual of earth follows, therefore we know that they're ready to relate something clever about him, and the spiritual man inside of the cavern. Both men have remarkable talents. The large cut emerald is starting to glow green rays of light. You've never seen them shed this much of the soft color. Aside the precious mineral and beneath it the warmth of its color is spellbinding. The explorer is out in front of the mine, looking back at the wide opening which has very beautiful golden light filling the insides now. The man and the mine are very miniature, and that's likely because of the changing scenery.

Many waxy yellow candles spread apart send a message of warmth in the light as small trails of light are still glowing in the background from a distance away. A circle of friends, mostly small children are returning on that strange cloud of whirling white light. What's up with that? They do command attention. Sure enough a yellow balloon, and a white balloon, and a blue one with a hand and a long string attached to each have children feeling happy. It's more of a day trip though. A young girl with brown hair and eyes, matching her tan teddy bear in her lap, gives him a big kiss. She is holding him tight. A tall door begins to open, and how wonderful the amazing white light is! More of this soft white light was beginning to surround each child, one at a time to show us that the Lord was apportioning it equally. Three baby angels in a v-shape sparkling are in gold at the bottom of the door. The little ones have circular white steering wheels to their ride. It's a gas for them. Are you becoming bored with these children? You shouldn't be. Make believe castles become real. The children see them blinking golden lights inside as they glide swiftly through the heavens in side of their spiritual vehicle of light.

Some of the castles are tall and white, and even many of them have more than just one garden, filled with colorful red, white and blue flowers to name just a few. The children will stop and smell them with delight. Many toy ponies sit in the front where green grass grows. A lovely woman who is the guide here at the special castle is sparkling in a lot of gold. She has shoulder length golden locks of hair. Her bonnet is black, and the tie beneath her chin fits her well as she is fancy free in nature. She has more of an open basket she carries over her left arm. You wouldn't question her, really, everyone knows she is there to watch over the children. A very small white kitten's face pops up over the basket. The young girl with brown hair is petting the kitten, but she left the ride, and the animal rests in a sitting position on a small white wave of light. The lovely woman wants it to be known how appealing her light brown dress with puffed out sleeves is. She does have style, not so out of date or old fashion. The cleanly look to her garment is amazing too. Four really big black clouds are growing a little larger as we speak.

They make one wonder if the second coming may be near, or if something even more astonishing is about to happen inside of the captivating heaven above. Onward with smooth sailing through life. An older gent of a sailor is standing on deck at the wheel of an earlier fisherman's vessel. His right eyebrow raises just enough to let you know that he means business when it came to manning the deck. His black raincoat and fastened back hat are soaking wet. There is a little bit more than meets the eye when it comes to rain in heaven then. The sailor turned his back on taking control of his ship now. Doesn't he care enough to stay on course with his life? But a gold cross is shining inside of his hand. He does appreciate the cross very much, so much that he folded his hands together for prayer, while it remained shining between them. The entire deck is filled with radiating sunlight from above, so much as that the clouds went away and the sailor removed his hat. But his brown hair is wet a tad. It was believed he asked God in prayer for a little sunlight in his life. He no longer could control the stormy weather nor his badly shaken emotions. But that's not all. At the same time, we were to understand that while we are to take control of ourselves, while at the wheel, we must overcome obstacles in life using only just a little bit of faith in prayer. First the sailor removed his raincoat and hat, abut now he places the coat on again. He even teaches other people valuable lessons about life, whether it be an actual skit played out, between the spiritual world and the physical level, or in heaven mostly, everything comes up smelling like roses again.

Wow, there are four pink vibrations of light that are totally of intelligible brilliance. As they have arrived, two across from each other, another vibration the pinkest color radiating below them comes after. Now a pink rose was centered inside of the divided areas of light. That goes to show you once again, the Lord knows what we are thinking about in the aforementioned and has contributed more to study. The pink vibes were more deep in color as each pink rose was lighter with prettiness. Inside of the area in between the light, which was earlier presumed to be empty, a glowing golden light is now spitting out sharp gold sparks which have landed in the center of each rose. Adding to their beauty is what Jesus wanted for them.

What may seem like the outline of a swooping slide, or a long curving design, was really the edge of the Lord's robe which carries Him along. It's possible to see Him in your home. There's a jetliner in orange light, brighter than what the sun would be providing as light on an object. At the cockpit there is a blazing fire burning out of control. The Lord's hands cupped together have reached beneath the airplane and what He did is nothing short of a miracle. Two women in a peach color vibration of circular light have been given an early retreat, unfortunately it came at a high cost to many aboard the wreckage. The Lord is also consoling many others who have finally been gathered in friendship. This was something that had occurred in the past. When it is your time the Lord will be waiting to love you abundantly. It's funny in a sense, all of the passengers aboard that airliner look very relieved. A common thread indeed. The passengers watched down below where their family and friends openly grieved their death. The dimensions of heaven and earth are different. It might seem like it will be a long time before you see your relatives again, but it is rather a short waiting period. Celebrate the happiness that they're feeling now.

We'll be aboard a few rides that will remind us of trains. But if you wish, it will be arranged to take a train ride if it pleases you. Do you wonder about swimming under water in heaven? Will you need to hold your breath while enjoying that activity? You'll think it is fun to watch your family and friends swimming beside you. You'll swim like a fish, and even think you'll be able to swim beneath clear water for a half of an hour at a time without having to catch your breath or fill up on oxygen. But we are able to blow small and larger bubbles beneath the water. You can see right through them. What else is allowed in the water? It's ok to say that, there are water instructors who'll offer you the chance to ride on dolphins by holding onto their large fin. Kids do have a lot of fun playing ball with the many dolphins. You'll be able to if you choose. They look exactly like the beach balls we have on our side, multi striped and colorful. But people in heaven may be instructed to swim within certain areas, without serious consequences though.

One of the things we'll learn about is why people died, wrongly. Even when we are seated and learning about what and why people were brought to heaven unexpectedly, you'll still feel like you're walking around on a marvelous vacation. The bliss of heavenly light surrounding your inner most being erases any doubt that you'll need to feel terrible about what may be heard from our lessons above. You can leave during the lessons at will which is nice of the Lord to allow. You'll be comforted by family every moment, that's how long eternity will feel. That duration extends way past what man has learned of in his time. Your voice will be much clearer to understand. When we lift our happy voice rejoicing with the Lord in heaven, it will be heard thus near and far. The angels will sing by your side as well. Funny as can be.

The largest whirling white light ride ever has come to a standstill for the moment. Kids keep popping up everywhere, wrapped inside of the clouded heavenly light, very much with a feeling of gladness in their hearts. Many of the children are black, white, Asian, and every ethnic background inside of heaven it seems. Many of the children have the v-neck tan and white robe being worn upon them. The light isn't a spinning wheel, however, it's so big and round, you'd never imagine little children being able to ride inside, outside, and on top of such a surprising spiritual shape created by the divine Masters.

Two trails of the white smooth light led to the gathering of children. Little gold stars are now part of the whirling of light. A curly haired boy with very light brown hair, along with numerous of the other adorable children branch off into a smaller version of the whirling white light ride in heaven. The lighted clouds, golden and white carry them off, but before a few of the remaining youngsters depart, one blue eyed girl with snow white hair, and pinkish cheeks takes a second look around, acting as a guide perhaps to make sure the coast is clear. She piggybacks her two fingers, because she is hopeful. A blue dash of light appears over her hand, signaling that a departure into the heavens is calling them closer now. Four children go off into their separate directions though. We know the heavens never end and run very deep. We have a slowpoke. A little boy wearing a black football helmet returns. Talk about front and center. Amazingly the small boy turned into a grownup too. From around the age of ten, to having the appearance of a thirty year old all at once. Wasn't that he is odd, because he grew like a giant suddenly, since he is in heaven, there's where miracles occur, what he experienced. He does have a football. It would be easy to offend some people on our side of life talking about the young man in such a manner, but in heaven the kingdom of God rules.

A white dove perched upon a gentleman's hand, suddenly flew away, and when doing so the tip of the bird's wing touches the tunnel of white light a distance away. But the soft dove doesn't fly directly through the beaming tunnel of light, but only goes out on his own. The dove was still covered by the light, since that's where it was last seen. The man's head was twice the size as a normal person's head would be. But since He favored Jesus in a paradisiacal spirit of Himself, we'll try to go along with the program once again. The mystical darker orange light which He arrived in with the dove was absolutely blissful. Enjoy your life in heaven.

You'll run like a deer when you're there, because of the lightness in your step, and the amazing coordination you possess. In comparison a runner wearing a real black uniform that racers use when they're on the track to run in is ready to lift up and run. He is within the presence of a small deer standing not two feet away. From one distance to another, if you choose to run fast or at a steady pace, you'll be surprised by the many unusual people who'll greet you. We'll have a path to follow. The simple life will be splendid. The festivals and merriment is overwhelming, although the happiness you'll endure will be good for your soul.

A very long dark road ahead seems to lead to nowhere, until a gold cross with emitting white light behind it whitens a pathway which is certain to make us happy. Golden cupped hands have merely scooped up the cross and pathway, but if we would like to see inside of the Lord's hands, and give Him our heart completely, He'll bring us into His own heart. You can see right through His hands, or what He has inside of them if that makes you feel any better. He holds an endless life in them. We are in His hands, even if we do fall by the wayside.

While the interpreter received a God awful kink in the neck, the outline of the physical self in spirit form was revealed. Why? First, a small marble size yellow dot appeared at the neck where the pain had flared up at. The one yellow dot near the midriff, and also inside of the leg area. This is sort of important information, especially for people with chronic pain who may need some healing done on their body. Each one of the dots expanded outward, and then inward it brightened in color. Picture the pain inside of your body leaving, after you have sent that very bright yellow dot away from the area which bothers you most. For some reason we can think of it as "God" color, and of a healing nature in the Lord's and our eyes. You know what? The pain is gone just because it was thought to be healed from the spirit's light source. It is kind of strange when you hear about these things, and then all of a sudden it works with yourself using the method. It may take a few times before the pain is gone, hopefully for good.

A spirit with snow white hair and unusual bangs for an older gent, presents himself wearing a long pointy beard and a very neatly trimmed mustache. His blue eyes are the clearest. He has the word "meditate" appear near his side. And while he is focusing in on meditation with his legs crossed a width of glowing yellow light enters into his spirit and brightens up inside of the center of his chest. Glowing streaked light reveals his face even more. You will receive peace from meditating like him. Now the dot is there and suddenly it is gone. The light of God from beyond is feather soft. By the way, a twinkling gold sparkle of light touches the mediator's nose.

Inside of the spirit world black and blue is more to the liking. A circle divided in half of these colors are spiritual symbols. A tall dark mountain appears a thousand miles up in the clouds, but surprisingly you can see an awe-inspiring blue sky below that. But why is there a mountain above the sky? Crumbling stones falling from topside tumble down the mountain, and after they have reached the bottom an unbelievable marker with neatly stacked rocks revealed three words, one on top of the next. It said, "Live Your Life."

The Lord just said, "Express yourself in the light." All we need to do is just put our best foot forward and we will succeed. No exaggeration, a lot of pure blue light appears everywhere. The heavens begin widening from each opening of these separate visions.

A gigantic city in heaven is full of golden churches with high steeples, along with arched bridges appearing the same, besides interesting streets in the same order. For what has been communicated, their way of life is enough to make you think twice about living again. A beautiful full rose, not as vibrant inside of the spirit as one would imagine, was elevated in mid-air, on an angle with a small leaf and thin stem. It's beauty was very heartfelt. Because if we look at that beautiful rose inside of a more vibrant light, which the holy spirit has done, setting a new flower out, we now see two of the same in a different ingenious form. On each side of a magnificent glowing gold tunnel of light, four yellow candles rest. From the bottom on up, they have increased in size. The Lord on a good side view is consoling His Mother, Mary, on His right now. Better than two days at the movies. A known white Christ light has dignified Her sparkling silver diamond studded crown much more. They are both pleased that we look up to them. Mary a beautiful spirit of a heavenly woman, known to have very lovely glimmering blue eyes wishes to keep them closed for the moment. Her long eyelashes are very brown. Many hats, some small and other varieties are larger, that's a surprising communication.

A bald man in the light, who you'd expect to have a full head of hair, is easily seen bending over. In a flash his scalp turned beet red. Even though he is inside of the holy spirit, under the Lord's, Father God's and Mother Mary's authority, he'll be a helpful guide in preventing serious problems up ahead, when we are outside under the sun without proper wear on our head. That is if you believe in messages from the other side of life. It isn't so ridiculous, just a reminder for your health. That man in the spirit has instant hair growth. It would be nice if we could market what he has, over here on our planet. His hair is jagged and brown, but he has captured our attention. A couple of bouncing white clouds are in view at about eye level. Another spiritual ride inside of the light perhaps? Remind the Lord that you're still waiting on the ride into heaven to occur, from your own personal experience inside of the whirling white light, that which is beyond the spoken word, but a joyous occasion that you are waiting to share with Him.

The pearly gates in heaven have opened up. Both of the large clouds have suddenly taken on a new form with someone on the other side of life attaching each cloud to the right and left side of its posts. Cleverly white flowers are in tact, and they hang down from the inner swirling design. First a small amount of gold light shined upon the lower area on the left side. Then the gateway turned gold, except for the flowers and the two clouds that were shown on the other side. With white flowers everywhere, everybody can still see right on through the gate that has just about closed all of the way, except for maybe a few inches. Did you think that God would close the gateway to His kingdom for good? And the Lord agrees with the communicator, also known as the "interpreter." An Indian wearing a white feather is warning of danger.

But that can be avoided. Don't be afraid he is only a guide to help us. He was giving the sign by holding up his hand to his mouth in speaking wisely to man below. On bended knee a spiritual Indian man, he will be forever and a day from now. The light of the holy spirit turned his feather white. After all, who are we to judge the color of a man's skin, or for what he was wearing?

Even the interpreter needs to pray for guidance, otherwise this wouldn't be happening. An experience of taking the fantastic whirling white light ride in heaven isn't enough, we need to know what else follows. How else would we know what to expect if we didn't see, hear and know what the holy spirit has to say? It's also very exciting not knowing what's coming up, it would spoil the big surprise they have in store for us. Step by step with out of body experiences, plus fun and entertainment inside of the light for one and all.

Visually there are several white plaques with glowing white edges. The kind you would love to touch, very opalescence. Someone was picking them up to show what's inside. Now they just want two of these glowing white objects to be used as examples. There were gold medals presented on the plaques in an upright position. A ruffled dark blue ribbon held them in place. An attachment for each. Were they really that? They believe it was an interesting enough question when asked. The other side insists "servers" deserve the medals. Also, for those who came into the light injured, people who were now deserving of such greatness. The medals are very rich looking. A nice gold star highlighted near a white and a pointed silver one are on a slant.

Why is the Lord and the Virgin Mary putting their crowns to rest? They sit side by side, His there on black silk, and Hers on white. Eternal speckles of silver light come from a much higher level, which were drizzling down upon Her diamonded crown. Golden richness fills the Lord's crown from a starlight and narrow light from above. Mary bends over. Sitting there in all of Her grandness, the Lord is setting the coronet upon Her ever so gently. Wow! Her crown is much taller than thought to be. And She is very big. She raised the Lord's stunning gold crown up and rests it upon His head ever so lovingly. That will be shared with you on the other side, too.

They're considerate enough to stand in the foreground of heaven, but the approach they've taken is highly unusual. Jesus and His Mother are both pointing upward, but outward too, up at where there is a white tunnel with a cloudy, scalloped, very overflowing entrance, away from where they stand. Many more of the white wrapped presents sit before the Lord and His Mother. And they have the same black bows. Some of these packages are small, but some are very large. The smallest one goes to someone on earth who has been reaching out to the Lord for help.

Two hands beneath the smallest gift wrapped present were close enough to touch the box. They're pleased you would ask for their help, and prefer that you would stand firm and be very eager to accept gifts of love from above. A woman in pure yellow light has now received her gift wrapped from our King and His giving Mother. The surprised look on the woman's face is amazing. She was floored just to receive the gift in her hands. But what did she receive? We shall see. Whatever that is it has to be big. We need to keep in mind that even though the woman is here on earth the present inside could be for her in heaven still. And it was. Inside of the box she pulled out a dazzling golden key. The woman has tremendous intuitive ability and can foresee what and how the key will fit into her future. She remains inside of the yellow soft light, but she turned her head and sees her very own gold castle in the distance.

Next a glowing white keyhole was shown. How the key suddenly popped into the keyhole in only a mere fraction of a second is mind-boggling. There are certainly two young angelic girls facing the castle with a flower bouquet in their hands. They wear stunning, lengthy white dresses, clearly of the finest spirit light, cloth, ever known of. Gleaming gold crosses light up the castle. They are on various angles, but they are beautifully representing the origin of life, where the surprised beneficiary will live her very long life. The lucky little lady is actually asleep, dreaming of her very own castle. She lays on her side in bed, that much is known from seeing her inside of the holy light. Her hands which are pressed together for prayer rest on the side of her face. Just because she is sleeping and experiencing an out of body experience into heaven where the Lord has given her a surprise gift, it's very likely, she was awaken inside of the dream state. Moving about in her dream came easy. You know it is true.

A family of four are trying to decide on what to do in the heavens, as they're covered in all white light, it was easy to determine the couple has two boys around the age of five, and they must be twins. The boys stand shoulder to shoulder at the same height. The woman is smelling a white lily flower, and simply admiring the golden hue from the inside. Funny how the flower is more visible than the family. They look like ghosts. The words "cloud nine" can be seen near the family of four. The woman's shoulders are dropping, to where she has touched the cloudy white heavenly floor, and much more easier to feel with her hands. There she points to two seeds used for planting. That is where we'll be growing with the Lord, no matter which way you look at her messages, she sought you out, not the other way around. Now a web of brilliant green vines are swirling throughout heaven, and finally new growth begins. The Master of all creation grew one sunflower, very bright orange, and much brown revealed in the center.

If the interpreter didn't know any better, the Lord just placed a very small two year old inside a whirling white light by His arms. And He certainly did. In front of the child, and in back of the wonder, three small golden balls of light mark off some of the territory, as though we were examining runway lights. It's truly amazing seeing the child resting on his back inside of a soft white crib made from the well willed light of God. It puffs up beneath his head. What's very hard to believe is that the Lord shows the boy inside of the spiral light, now resting in the palm of His hand. But the appearance of the little one changes, to where he was observed more closeup, while firmly established as he laid in a comfortable nest of spiritual light. But the child is being shifted around the whirl of light, first from the middle, to the higher right side, and then to below, where he is still very much at peace in the hands of the Lord. Each stop the boy had made created a powerful bright white light glow. The birthplace of this child is in heaven, spiritually that is.

A smiling baby boy is very clear, and talking about in good health with those rose red little cheeks. You just want to love him. The child is being handed back and forth between two women covered in the light. They have shoulder length hair with curls galore. The woman and her friend have finally come to light clearer, as they have beautiful pink cheeks. The taller gal kissed the baby on his right cheek, leaving a perfect imprint of red lipstick. Surprisingly, she had wiped off the lipstick immediately using a very fine and delicate cloth she was holding onto.

There is gold light in heaven and more of it. Why so much of the gold? Even as it flows like honey through the air, you have to wonder. Liquid gold with silver sparkles enlighten some, so it is believed from the design it brings. In heaven you become overwhelmed with peace, a special feeling stimulated from love. Three children wearing black and white helmets are beginning to enjoy a special race. They will be guided carefully. They have to go along with the rules, there will not be any harm to any of the other drivers. It sounds so mature up in heaven, but without instructions or healthy advice, they wouldn't have anyone of such grand authority ruling over them with love. Inside of a partial golden light, someone's index finger is pointing to three special areas, where even more gold vibrations of color exists. Those are places to where the very youthful drivers inside of their derby cars enclosed with whirling white light are foreordained. They are off and gliding with ease. Out from the corner of the Lord's right eye, on a side view of Him, He can see the kids way out and about, captured inside of much more peaceful golden light. You can imagine how far they have driven already from how little they appear such a distance away. But in the Lord's eyes, they're as close as you and I are.

You may enjoy aligning your eyesight, to where you'll now be able to see two bright blue circles of light glow before your very eyes. It would surprise you to learn that you are a prodigy. There are times when you can see what is going on in heaven, through the subsequent learning process. That would be a thrill to be an observer and absorb. Concentrate on the blue spiritual light. Beyond the blue eternal presence a tall tree with sparkling orange leaves sits next to a lake you'll want to know much more about. Deep in your mind, using your spiritual eye within, capture the beauty of nature in heaven. The distance of the setting may seem far to you, but going there and being closer inside of the heavens will give you an idea how peaceful it is. Gold leaves fill the other trees nearby, it feels like summer, it feels like spring. And you know something? You'd want to die there if you could. The truth of the matter is you can't pass away with the holy spirit within your soul. We will remain free forever. Yes there are water skiers there who think you'll have the time of your life. You'll be encouraged to join in the fun with them. You can bet your bottom dollar on that if you want. You should believe that you need to feel comfortable about the way you'll be expressing yourself in heaven, without the fear of condemnation. Freedom is considered a luxury. But the Lord has a secret about how we control our speech. Some people are afraid of the power which exists in the Lord and Father God.

"I can tell you are interested in my well being," came from inside of the holy spirit, using visible dark lettering. The words were fancy in design. An artist would be absolutely jealous of the Lord's creative abilities. Was it God or Jesus who spoke? That was a communication from both. The spirit moves calmly inside of the holy light because they're taking interest in us. Between numerous pure gold angels, who'd remind you of statues, yellow brightens. One has a clam shape dish filled with fresh water in front of its wings, nearest to its foundation. And the angel on the left tilted a u-shape harp in between them with outstanding movements. The strings are in tact. Over to the left, an angel with a cute trumpet. Evidently it is being used. That special angel's right wing glistened more than his companions. Anything to get your attention, those silly angels. To follow, the next one on over to the left has a small thin gold cross at the edge of its wing. A barely visible thick white stocking with a ball at the top was seen, and the ornamentation almost puts one into the Christmas spirit all over again. Two very embellished sparkling gold balls to hang on a tree represent themselves before the angels. They sparkle more around the middle, leaving a mirrored image of lighter gold to the tops and bottoms. Now a marble size tunnel of light seems to be a mile away, in front of the many angels. Instantly a shining gold sparkle of light shined on the interpreter's left hand. The signs will exist with most everyone on the planet, different as they may be at times. And the changes inside of the holy spirit are good.

The softest snow you ever have seen exists in heaven. The snow capped mountains will make you speechless. The puffy white stuff is cleaner and much easier to walk upon. The skiers will leave many swerving trails behind them in this event endured. There's the skier, a man inside of a tucked position, ready to snow ski, but what he is ready to partake in is much more similar to an extreme sport which some people over here risk their lives doing. The mountain is high, and he turns his head and shifts himself sideways a little bit to reveal that he is really there basking inside of a soothing amber light. He pointed to the tip of one of his skis as the spectrum of light shows him much more, distantly, but still atop the mountain. The skier is dropping straight down, but he is enjoying the activity very much so. He finally hit a snow drift, and that great big smile remains on his heavenly face. Funny, his cheeks seem redder than someone in heaven would probably have, although he is traveling fast inside of the spirit world, there is nothing telling of him being cold. With his poles and hands dropping to his side something uncanny develops. Both of the skis he is wearing are now sticking out from the inside of a whirling white light. It forms rolls of thick cloudy light around his neck, and especially his waistline and his feet.

The power of the God light is pulling him somewhat backwards, to where the enthusiastic young man is almost laying flat. Then without notice he is pulled forward, and now he turns clockwise, where the back of his head filled with brown hair is showing. He seems to be all set in place, not wrapped up like a mummy, but experiencing an extraordinary feeling of joy. His skis slip off, beneath the light they have been set aside, sticking straight up in the middle of a small snowbank. He'll be departing, but not without us knowing where to. Three beautifully glowing white balls of white light are shafts of some sort. That's where he points to. One is way out to the right side of heaven, then he's signaling down below, where the other glowing lit shaft of light is, and then he will travel out and upward to the left side inside of the heavens.

He wants to give the route some features. Funny how he is allowed to do so, from handling the ball size of glowing blue light in his hands. He is looking straight at it, while sending the image of it out to each location using his mind. But each of the white shafts of light now have a large blue plume above the openings. In front of the spiritual man who enjoys teaching us new things about heaven are many incandescent lights forming a variety of see-through doors.

For the most part the man will appear soon. He has and the pacesetter pointed to the distant shaft of light, similar to a ball of white light, that which has a large blue hue. But he is faster than the dickens and has already made it there, and then he pointed to where he was again, over on the left side of heaven. But he played a little game with us, he didn't scoot down below, he had earlier pointed out the path, but he chose how he wanted things done his own way. From the other side of life he is making his inspections. Now completely turned around, facing us on earth, he has the one rounded ball of white light which has incredible value to him, and the world rests beneath his hands, as his fingers and palms lay upon the very top of the lasting opening.

He whirls inside of the peaceful white light. He is also happy to make our acquaintance. A gold cross taller than the man appears. The man's head is closer to the bottom of its structure, but he enjoys being able to feel the God presence close by. His whirling white light is producing sparkling gold at the top, around the middle, and now around the entire lower area. He knows that we can and should understand what he is doing for us. His eyes turn brown. The whirling white light ride which he took us on evaporated. That can't be entirely true though. But for the meantime, there wasn't a sign of him being engaged with the ride. But he does stand here inside of the spirit world, dressed very debonair in a sparkling floor length golden robe which seems to be new outerwear. For cufflinks a small gold cross glows at the bottom of each sleeve. A white one glows ever so softly upon his chest.

Egg shape reflective light in the spirit becomes a mystery. Though the shape and color are pretty and quite pearly more intuitiveness will be necessary now. It certainly wasn't an egg, but still food for thought mentally. Now one becomes stacked upon the other pearly image of light, leaving a unique sight in comparison to a footpath, one that would shine and lead us into the future. There really is someone in the light giving a "thumbs up." No wizardry here, all spirituality and we're just sticking to the Almighty's plan. Yes we'll be wondering where the path will lead us, until the time is right for the Lord to instruct with His holy visions and unquestionable judgment. Pinkish orange light is coming to view, and since it did at that, clarity inside of the heavens is tremendous.

Inside of the light, the orangish pathway has a hospitable visitor stepping up holding a huge cake in his hands. The candles which decorated the frosted cake were quickly counted, but since they were so close together, second thoughts were given to the exact number. But what was very helpful was the number "eleven" appearing on the other side. And we are about to hear why. The candles are white with yellow lights for flames. On top of each flame sparkling silver brightens. The cake is white that's for sure, and every couple inches or so a red rose decorates the outer edge. With the arched grey grave marker inside of the light it is obvious that in heaven people who were involved with the September eleven event are looked upon in the highest regard. And in heaven is where we celebrate freedom and know inside of our hearts that we will never feel harm again. The party goes on in heaven for those who were favored to be united with the Lord. It has just been informed people who lost their life have joined together to celebrate the Lord. A grey cloud in the sky just turned gold too. The Lord is happy.

Why do you think a small rounded gold coin just dropped inside of a black slot? It has to be a ride coming up. You name it, black, red, blue, and white balloons are floating through heaven. A gold track with black ties across the structure suggests a railway. But wait a minute! A little boy is riding inside of a black train car. No, it wasn't an illusion. He has a second car, that says "coal" on the side. The image of a small girl in white light is obvious, because she is seated inside of a third car. A copper color large wheel under the train has a spot of white in the center of it, which now substantiates the children are on track and have agreed upon a trip together. Where are the rest of the kids? The little girl has company. Her white bunny rabbit with cute shiny brown eyes is stuffed, but to her, he or she may be real with an adorable name. There wasn't a fourth car attached to the train. But how very cute they are in heaven. Puffs of cloudy white light were left in the air in the shape of hearts. The little boy in the engineer's car has several controls in front of him on a lit panel. And how is it that Jesus is sitting casually inside of the light glancing at the children? He owns the heavens. And with His hands reaching out to the children in a cupped manner, which we have belief in, He has that repeated giving side that will not fail. The white bunny rabbit is being shown to a crowd of children who are watching near the track with their parents. The number of children in heaven is wildly uncanny, but you know they are there for a reason. In wonderment the kids seem to enjoy the boy and girl whizzing by, while waving and cheering them on with cute smiling faces, brushed with the delicate golden light.

Ivory wing angels floating about even have a fluffed ruffle about themselves, surrounding the train cars, but at a suitable distance very majestical. Another funny thing happened in heaven today. A curly headed boy with golden hair aims a solid gold arrow of light from his u-shape harp, sending it forward to the young girl riding along the railway. She opened up a piece of paper to read now. Turns out she is keeping her message more of a secret. She took the evenly creased down the middle piece of paper and pressed it close to her heart. She is very well dressed in a white dress. Her wonderful head of brown curls shows, and the red bow in her hair is large, surprisingly. The boy angel who sent her the important message has gold wings. Unbelievable for his size, considering they are attached to his shoulders with the arch. The front of the engine is moving forward now. A white glowing light from the front is something special. And there are two smaller white lights on each side of that one.

Without not as much beam they are still on. The engineer stopped the train. He is walking down a small staircase that leads to the surface of heaven. He has taken hold of a small railing to assist him on the side of the train. If the boy wanted to he could probably just float on outside, and then inside of the mellow golden light in which they're surrounded by. And what a little gentleman he was. The lad went to the third car to help her down from the ride. He held his hand out to take hers. The kids have an invigorating movement

95

in their stride. You'll be happy to know that the children have both brought their hands to their mouth to giggle, and only if we could try and be like them we would be extremely happy then. The children have found their way to a place where they'll sit under a sensational canopy of light. The orange light beneath their feet goes well with the cover above them, shaped identically to a gigantic smooth leaf of a much different shaded color. Tan starfish are scattered upon a ton of sand. The bright yellow strap handles on white pales for the children have given them easy access for handling. They're squatting and scooping up sand into them now. Small ripples of water come flowing in on shore which makes it easy for them to shape objects. These kids are far more advanced than we are, and both eagerly study closely the sand castle that they have almost finished in the sand. It has only been a minute or so, that's in our time, whereas they have already built a three foot high castle applying meticulous workmanship. Let's try and let them be at peace where walls of bright pink flowers pop up close by. They just hang down, the beautifully shaped arrangement. Too beautiful for words, but easy on the eyes and memory.

You wouldn't have thought it were true that other people in heaven close to the Lord wore a gold crown. Perhaps the many young children who were seen had been awarded one, similar to our Lord's very own crown. Likely we will witness that someday in attendance at such a ceremony. Their crowns are the same color as the Lords, but more mild looking and very light weight to wear. Mostly the boys have one. Does Father God wear a crown? It sure is big and silver. And if you like rubies, there's one in the center of His crown that would make an honest man want to steal it away. But that wouldn't be a good idea, after all, God just revealed a crown with the royal highlight embedded into such wonderful silver.

Just ask Him in prayer to show you the crown of God Almighty. Look up and you shall see such prominence. The Lord wouldn't be offended if you pictured yourself wearing a gold crown. You'd be surprised if He let you wear His for a moment or two. He wants some of the children to wear one for play. The royalty they feel is grand.

An important figure arrives. She is accompanied by two young girls, who're now lifting the bottom edge up to the woman's very silky white dress as she walks. The girls have brown hair with the becoming braid wrapped around. The woman's helpers have matching dresses, such as her own, but they have a large bow tied in front. And it wasn't who the interpreter thought. Long brown hair sweeps back and past this royal figure's shoulders, and you can guess by now who it is so renowned. Probably why the mistake was made was because of His robe being thought of as a long dress. But when the small branch and thorn filled wreath was focused in on upon our Highness, there was a slight feeling of embarrassment from being temporarily out of touch. Though that only lasted a minute. A thin but sharp blue ray brings forth light. Although black candles may not be very popular, in heaven they are sitting before a very deep blue background of light, each one not shining any particular color of light as flickering fire would. They teepee, one on each side with one present on top. A choir boy over to the left comes in on a side view with him preparing to light each dark candle. The image of the boy is of him covered in white light, evenly proportioned. But he is surprising. The boy steps up, reaches out to one candle at a time, with his back turned, bringing his hands almost all the way together, he left enough room to watch the glowing flame of light ignite between them. He glows and the light does brightly. There was just enough space between his face and his hands to see that every black candle was lit differently, and not by using an ordinary match either. He prayed for light and it was given. First candle received an orange light of fire, the following on up was white, and the next was just gold sparkles. Even though the holy spirit moves him back a distance away, there was the image of the choir boy meditating for more light to be given. And before we forget, at each interval an extra rounded white ball of light began glowing, nonstop, behind every lit candle, including the special golden wick at the very top.

The baby angel boy with black hair, sitting on top of the whirling white light that glows in gold at the bottom is in peace. But with the same whirling white light on each side of him a holistic feeling has transcended over normal thinking. That little stinker is pointing down over the edge of the swirl of light, to where a golden image of a floppy eared dog rests beneath him. A hazy white tunnel up away from the boy raised him and his friend into the approaching eternal light. Somehow the dog left the boy's funny cloud and has come in contact with people who seem to be taking turns petting the animal. The baby boy is literally at arms length of the Lord. Relax in the light as it softens. An eager woman on the other side of life is grooming the dog with a brush which has golden bristles. Down the coat she goes, back and forth, smoothly. The dog's tongue is hanging out. It's quite pink, maybe just because of the brilliant life and color in heaven, most likely. But that doesn't quite answer a question we were trying to figure out. What happened to the huge white light mass in the heavens that was surrounding the baby angel and dog? The Lord has the ride reserved for the next guests of honor coming to greet Him. One might be for you and your friends. The sooner that very peaceful and unfailing whirling white light ride returns the better. A whirling feeling that keeps your head on straight. Look at the kid and his dog. If you're still laying in bed awake at night waiting for your ride, and it hasn't come just yet, you're not praying hard enough. Silly as a real heaven? Loving that ride.

It's the difference between day and night in heaven and earth, us with all of our daily worries, but while we enjoy the other side, we'll be more carefree. You need to give credit where it is due, no doubt of that when it comes to the Lord trying new things. A perfect image of Him inside of the fascinating cloud He was creating became visible and a little alarming. Not the kind of cloud where you would see the image of a man blowing air or hot smoke out from inside, but a holy sight with decorative golden balls of light on the upper and lower corners. Without any difficulties arriving inside of His holy spirit, we shall enjoy where He ushers us.

The Lord would rather we didn't feel like we were on the spot in life with our feelings. Just start anew. Why would the Lord want us to picture the white light over our heads with our eyes closed right now? That's what He was instructing. Why not give it a go? He thought while showing the light that it is best to think of it as wide and very thick. See it as a simple test from the spirit world. You may think of it as white as snow if you would like. Don't let any other thoughts interrupt you from meditating. Let your mind be free from worry. It is being translated, actually from the spirit language of God. Now we must go through short intervals of picturing the snowy white light with our eyes open, and then doing so the other way around with our eyes closed. Now seek out the whirling white light in the midst. What was the Lord doing? His hand appeared beneath His chin, with Christ appearing more like flesh color, but as a holy spiritual Lord. His presence is close by and visible how He prefers in spirit. The gold crown appears upon His head now. That was a sudden change, since we should understand, that when He does come in and out of the spirit, He is inclined to change His appearance, regardless of what some people may be thinking. There will always be something special about Jesus.

The Lord holds an opened gold timepiece in His right hand to examine the time. Maybe there is some time in heaven after all. It is everlasting at least. He shows what time it is. The clock reads exactly one o'clock. But He doesn't reveal night or daytime. One in spirit is the right message. You'd have to see the timepiece in his hand, practically touching His white robe, while casually being held, to be more pleased. His hand moved so fast that the timepiece, not only disappeared, but it dematerialized with the goldest sprinkles being let loose from the Lord's hand. When they reached heaven's solid foundation, where the Lord is presently standing, the sprinkles turned softer, bringing a glowing sensation of golden light upon the Lord's feet. Purple aside blue bubbles seem to just bubble outwardly. Sort of like liquid light, if that makes any sense at all. Very pretty to look at. Jesus is taking care of people, the spirit is unveiling many going ons inside of the holy spirit. And as such, three people on their knees in golden light are praising the Lord effortlessly. The words "you're excused" appear in black lettering near everyone present. The Lord is responding to them, and also down to earth for all to hear.

The brightest white light we will ever see inside of the heavens shimmers with stateliness. Above it a cyclone shape cloudy white light is starting to form. Could it be? The one and only "whirling white light ride in heaven," again? You bet your booty it is, and the light separated, forming two split rides. One on the right side of heaven, and the other on the left. Don't be afraid, because they'll never confuse us with distorted facts.

A sweet little Asian boy is laying flat on his tummy, but on top of the gradual moving light. There he goes sliding down a curling strip of lengthy white light, as though he were on a sled. A solid circle of blue light glows above the boy while he enjoys gliding about, and suddenly the heavens around him turn all blue. Calmness has always been within his presence. He ended up where a cloudy white landing secures him in place. He is resting on his tummy still and contented. He would like us to look back at where he came from. You wouldn't believe that he just twisted his left hand and wrist slightly in a short wave. Now for sure, he is waving to someone back at the starting point. The second cloud of whirling light moves gradual and steadily it is traveling down the same brighten white path of light that is dipping into the heavens. Someone is definitely on the ride, but only half of the person's face is showing from behind the top edge of the curled up form of light. The whirling white light is getting brighter and visibly forthcoming, and from examining the outer existing layer, the light begins bulging. Someone seems to be nudging against the inside. Now the image of an unborn child appears to be resting inside of the light, able to be seen in the formation of white light too.

The whirling light begins to glow some gold on the bottom while going down and down inside of heaven. The traveling light cloud stopped. The unborn child inside has turned gold, but mostly in a softer version. A small Asian girl with very dark hair and pretty brown eyes positioned herself behind the infant, caring very much about the safety of the child. Now face forward, which is totally remarkable to be witnessing, the girl is looking at the child and up at the interpreter. She has awaken the infant. So the child was born after all. In heaven that would be right. But the infant has been moved to the opposite side of the cocoon of holy light. And what she did next was beautiful. She held the child up near her side. Now she is with a baby boy. He was dressed in a tan color soft robe. She has on a heavily pleated white dress. The blue light in the background appears darker but colorful. The children from the other rides are looking back at the scenery. The heavens have offered endless opportunities for the children, this is why you are learning something that you should be finding "not hard" to swallow.

Before you know it all three children are together. The boy and the girl are watching the infant resting, and he lays there in such joyous accord sucking on a baby pacifier. That was unexpected. The girl is laying back inside of the white ride, now behind the two boys, who have departed a little bit ahead of her. But the dark haired girl ends up above them now, smiling down upon them, not in a mean way. They are fast. Funny how they have stopped in an area just gleaming with a huge spread of gold light surrounding them with warmth. And a woman leans forward inside of the light and takes the baby from the boy, while handing him over from his arms to hers. Both of the light travelers are outside of the ride and given a silver chalice of drink. The young Asian boy started sipping first before the girl. And it appears the drinks were clear as water, and just may have been that. A faithful man of God who was dressed in a fine black tux, pants, and a white shirt is also wearing a white bow tie. He was handed the chalices, which were set upon a silver tray, that he served them with. Is he the butler? A servant was he, and while the gent faithfully looks upward into the heavens holding firmly onto his silver tray, a twinkling silver star appears above his head. Can you believe what they do up in heaven at any given moment can be similar or just like this? It's found to be accommodating.

A very beautiful angel, really big in size, nestles the two children closely. And the angel is a woman too. Her halo is snow white, and even sparkling gold which made a deep crease inwardly. With eyes of blue, she is hypnotic. You can see one of the little boy's hands and the girls. They both seem to be blowing a kiss in the wind. Not too good to be true, but very interesting children from the other side of life would act like this in the presence of the heavenly angel above, and toward people seeking out truth from them in a much higher conversant level of life.

The holy spirit is a marvel to be appreciated from their view on life. There are hundreds of things to do in heaven at any given moment. Experienced teachers there will inform us what to do. A petite young lady around thirty comes forward. In a sparkling gold light covering her from head to toe, what stands out most of all are the small black flowers in her hair. Inside of her hands was a white vaporous cloudy light, where she hand picks one of the small stemmed black flowers from the inside. She adjusts a flower neatly to the front of her hair, and with the others in place, she instantly created a flowery wreath. A small ball of smooth white light which often shines, does so first softer then brighter. She shows that there is a small wand in her hand that turns different colors and shapes. The wand is tan, but the top is a gold star. It turns into a black ball on top, without her telling us why that happened. We would still want her on our side if all the time we had left in life to live was forty five seconds.

This will be described in the light. A black ball is bouncing, down a staircase that continues sloping in a curling shape. The little ball also slides a bit, before the bounce. The creation of the narrow stairway is simply remarkable, because of the ball moving so rapidly. It was more like a ball being guided on a long dark string with many ups and downs. A young Indian girl squatting at the bottom in her deerskin dress, wearing a dark red feathery headband, scoops up the ball into her hand. She seems to be counting, using hand gestures, raising the ball up and down inside of her hand, ready to toss it up into the heavenly air. On the count of three the ball flies up into the air and turns itself into a white ball of light. Funnier than the day is long, she reaches up to the white ball of light and watches it turn solid black in color. You know who she reminds us of? The wand carrier earlier whose gold star turned into a black solid color. All things considered, they are associated with each other inside the kingdom of our Lord and Almighty God.

A bright yellow turtle is crawling along in the light with a skinny number "one" on its shell. Where is the green? If we take away the eternal light of God shining so brightly, we'd probably notice its earthly color more. At the top of the number you couldn't help but notice a small ring of white light with some sort of darkness on the upper rounded edge. Either they have cartoons up in heaven, otherwise we are certainly in for a big surprise with this fella. His neck looks bigger while he lifts his head up as to be examining everything around him very close. He acts like he knows what the interpreter is thinking, that smart. He continues to crawl away into a curious area of numerous small white bead bubbles that have formed firmly around him.

But we can fix our attention even more on the light. Ruby red and canary yellow eternal rays of light burst in the heavens, highlighted with many arches of golden sparkles, very much like fireworks going off. Even white bursts of light rays manifesting silver sparkles. You can count on much more than that. Their fireworks would be more for entertainment value.

One soft white angel's wings comes in the light, then a ball of white light, then the same occurred. A gold picket fence with golden flowers hanging loosely is above the forming angel. A full golden arch of a halo is covering a half side to one of the balls of light. Someway the unnatural angelic wing attached itself onto the white rounded color of light. Two brown eyes appeared. Is this angel being created right now? Yes! The Lord can do most anything, and He will tell you that. What was that coming from the angel's eyes? Drizzling golden sparkles extended from the angel's eyes touch a young boy's opened hands. He is beneath the angel, but a seeker in the light who has his hands full of this extremely bright, and very soft transcendental light form. The angel's eyes have something new. A gold star above each eyebrow. The angel moves into another source of light. The young child blows into his hands, watching the golden sparkling light shoot upward, and he sees four matching gold ponies on a merry-go-round ride. And as the light featured boy takes his turn on the ride moving around, his guardian angel, the one created from inside of heaven was riding along right behind him. Acknowledge that the angel was girlish, and besides being fond of the boy, she'll make us all wonder how God did that. He took His own creation of light and brought forth an angel. God creating people in angelic form has to be very rich. But why not just sit back and enjoy the rest of the show?

Hard to accept for some perhaps, however, women can apply mascara to their face in heaven. There is a heavenly soul of a beautiful woman applying eyeliner right now. She wants others to know it's similar to what you think. And they are homebodies in the heavens. Television might sound a little farfetched, but there really are many shows in heaven that we will all like. If it is baseball that you like, in no time at all, up there you can play the game or watch it from the sidelines. Life is so easy in God's kingdom that you'll laugh. And why we wonder if we should feel more at ease, feel convinced. Purple lilacs in a softer than usual white cloudy light. Visible just now inside of heaven. A reminder of what they mean to us, a part of our lives.

A white tornado with a pink hue is spinning faster than any of the white light rides would do. Once it stopped the pink color fluffed up, where the Lord in spirit created a delectable ice-cream cone. It was a surprise to learn of such a treat in the hereafter. He has much more to relate about that, there's no way He wouldn't comment somehow inside of the spirit world. Three white swirls of delicious ice-cream appeared on a silver tray. Just two hands and a golden light are visible up to this point, but it is likely that the butler or one of the servants is holding onto the sides of the tray. Little hands again. They are reaching up to the server's tray for their treat which was being offered out to the children. What seems odd or small happens to be bigger than life, especially in the Lord's eyes, He loves children so much. The kids walked up to a white counter where a long haired blonde woman is bending over with a scoop of brown and blue candy sprinkles. With such a light hand she tops off each cone for three, and faster than anyone you've ever seen anyone do it in any ice-cream parlor anywhere in town.

Even though the heavenly server of treats behind the counter is inside a distant light of the Lord, her long apron was nicely decorated with yellow flowers. The two golden crosses may appear smaller than they are, one by the white tunnel of light and the other, right next to the planet earth, an exciting visual from the holy spirit. If the Lord happens to repeat Himself on occasions it was to verify His whereabouts. The Lord is saying, "I am patient with you." Naturally His words were seen in the spirit, formed as such. The calmness in His words and voice are loving. He would like us to leave the "bad" alone when we can. You know when you have a day when you have to take a double take? A triple take here. A tall humpback camel, a golden scroll with a black tie, and nothing but a dry desert land. Since when do they have camels in heaven? Probably since yesteryears gone by. Land will be "ours" when residing with the Lord and our Father God. The scroll unravels and it only has one word spelled out in bold black letters, stating, "Peace." As how the word was represented on the golden parchment. To see that message revealed without spotting anyone present to open the scroll was hard to believe. As if a gust of wind blew it open in midair. The camel has rested on all fours.

A small sandstorm in the heavens have whipped up a couple of twisters. Why would that happen? The Lord isn't violent. He was on His throne, then He got up in a hurry, rushing back and forth in front of His throne like a nervous Father waiting on the birth of His child. Jesus was concentrating on each index finger on each of His hands twirling the sand about. And you wonder, could that be? The twister on the right was dominated downward, smaller and smaller, until finally it created a small sand castle. Jesus must be a kid at heart in a sense. The kids create them in a snap, and so can He. The other wonder of spinning sand rotates slower, but on top of the Lord's hand now. The sight of it finally changes, and surprisingly as clever as the Lord is, He turned the sand into another sand castle to rest mainly upon His hand.

For fun they'll decide when the whirling white light ride comes, but until then, why don't we all just go to heaven. Sitting in his chair a young man covered in white light is becoming more brighter through his eyes, as he draws our attention to a cloud, that which he holds between his hands. Let's hope he is magical. Spiritually, we are on his side in thought, and if you see him, if you're that highly educated to believe in the light, during this moment, watch how he behaves for a minute. He tries to spin the white cloud of light, but finds it almost impossible. Hard to believe that since he's quite mighty himself. His eyes are large and oval, and they have changed to gold. And a small gleaming white light inside the center, where his pupil belongs is close to freaking the interpreter completely out of his mind. But logic says that spirit people, far advanced as they are have an outmaneuvering way about themselves. It may not be intentional, but to make us put on our thinking cap. Find the center of his eyes appearing before you. Go ahead, you're not being brainwashed. You'll like the way you sense him inside of the holy spirit.

The sitter was given the Holy Bible, in gold print mind you. Quite a nice cover. He points up to the white tunnel of light, which is shedding not only upon himself, there are people rejoicing inside of the peaceful state too. A straw manger and a red heart gleaming in soft pink light are symbols the Lord desires to relate directly to us. The Lord enlightens us with messages about His birth. He says, "God had a crown waiting for Me. Love your neighbor." Only if it was as easy as He tells us. But we shall try, and He'll leave it up to us to think of others the same way. Don't worry, when He speaks to others in heaven we'll all be wondering what He was saying, therefore, leaving no doubt whatsoever that the Lord is able to speak to anyone, anywhere, at any given moment. He is being more than reasonable with the interpreter and the crowd of listeners.

All of the colorful and most meaningful ribbons in the colors of yellow, red, blue and pink are part of the scenery shown. And now a red ribbon comes in the light, reminding us that God has not forgotten about people on our side of life who've suffered with specific illnesses. He supports by standing behind people with aids as well. It was good thinking on His part to convey that, just in case we have someone out there today who feels that God doesn't care about what they have been going through with their health. There is hope. Funny, God is beautifying His immediate surroundings with four white bows. The Lord has very dark eyebrows, which He is pointing out to us, the reason why would be because He is raising His right eyebrow into an arch. He feels that this information, past, present and in the future will be raising eyebrows. How can one not agree with His friendship thus far? He is happy about who He is visiting with, and especially with us. But His people in heaven are very important so don't feel upset if the stage is all His right now. He is placing children back and forth from sitting on His lap, back to where they were gathered before Him at the throne. Or in front of Him. He is wonderful to watch.

When you look into heaven the beauty of the friendly people and settings becomes eye catching. Everyone and everything will grab your attention. We may think that the light from heaven is old news, but really it is still as fresh and enlightening as the day is young. We will find a way to expand into the light for the thrill of it.

There's that black wiggling line again. Another way to reveal a pathway in life, and in heaven does exist. A shiny black harp is being played by an enthused spirit friend. Her strings are tall and they sparkle in gold from across the top of the harp connecting down below. A group of musicians now are sitting with their solid orange, soft yellow, and even a yellow harp. The people playing rapturous music feel they bring peace to those who enjoy song. Three kids take shape in and on their white light rides of puffy clouds. They listen to the harpists and understand what is being played. The children have funny attire. One child wears a pink and white robe, colored, half and half. Pink on the left side and white on the right. And the other kids, the same style, but colors of yellow and white, and blue and white. Beginning of amazement.

A man in the spirit with a very long nose takes a bow. Nothing personal with the facial feature, but if you saw it you'd really be surprised by its length. His hair is very white and curly. His head is huge. It's hard saying yet if He's trying to be funny or what. He is smelling the white carnation on His robe right at the moment. He wants us to hold. We have intervened with Him in a way with all of this spiritual communicating in His world now. He doesn't feel we are being rude, we just took Him by surprise. Lucky Him with the rose red cheeks. His head is turning. His beard is soft as silky hair. A small twinkling gold star shines on the edge of His fine beard. But why did His facial hair, including the mustache all turn gold? But His face remains the same, at least for now. Something different about Him too. The second time around when He changed, just His head was visible. He went somewhere, but Jesus is here in His place.

There He stands wearing a long white robe. He tugs at a neatly creased handkerchief in a pocket near the top of His garment. When He moved it a bit a gold cross appeared as an emblem. The crown upon His head is pure white. Hey, He's in heaven directing spiritual lessons. Our first guest actually wasn't Jesus, unless it was God again, expressing Himself inside of the Lord's spirit, whereas when Jesus stepped forward, the Lord knew that anyone who could make just their head appear had to be Supreme. At first it was thought that the Lord was shrugging His broad shoulders. A second look at Him inside of His holy spirit revealed a pretty angel with heart shaped ivory wings lifting and then resting in place. The angel wearing a long pearl necklace picks it up at the bottom, and she gently kissed one. A bowl with a gleaming gold rim tilts forward. It isn't that deep, but the angelic woman has it full of extra pearls. The beautiful angel, besides having ivory wings, she comes in a decorative grey robe, and it doesn't seem to be a sin at all for the females to wear white carnations, the same as the Lord would and many of the gentleman. Sworn to God, she lifts the carnation to her nose for a good smell.

Let's hope that the dark grey deep sea dive helmet, and all of the whirling white light brings us to an important place. Revealed in the heavens a diver has gone beneath a spiritual surface of thick white clouds and light to begin an adventure, one that will have to be passed on to many. He gives the "victory" sign with his left hand, using two fingers. To some it would be the peace sign. His cheeks are getting fatter. The expression is of one who is holding his breath beneath water, but that can't be what our gentleman friend in the light is doing. Funny, he is slowly rotating clockwise in a fairly decent size circle. How strange seeing him and the large helmet whirling around inside of the thick white light. You want to say "weird," but we're dealing with the holy spirit still. With his rotation, he manages to release a bubble, glistening in a golden clear light inside, that appears on each side of the large area, and above and in front of the man. Under water there is pressure, but not in the light. The diver has left the whirling light and is beginning to remove the helmet. His face has either warm sunlight or a saffron light upon him. With a clinched fist against his heart it looks like he is having a heart attack. He flattens his hand to avoid any confusion, while he smiles freely. He and the Lord change the scene. The Lord certainly was involved. Inside of a gold light, which was becoming dim, why, that hasn't been determined yet, is where many people were inside of deep water reaching up to the Lord for help. And instead of swirling water sucking them under a white light of the holy spirit slowly begins to stir. It whirls clockwise around each person. Young men and women appearing to be Asian are obviously still wet though. They are sitting comfortably in heaven with the glimpses of light that are beginning to brighten more at the crossing. The top of a roof from a house is floating on water with sunshine covering it. God's house is built strong for all people to join in unity with Him. Sink or swim, God knows your name. We might even say that God is the "deep sea" diver, One who can save anyone in a time of need, any day of the week.

Some more elevation of the mind to receive more from heaven should do just right about now. You have to think quick when accepting great visions on this side of life. Coming from the Lord, a little boy with a golden spoon in his hand is whipping up a big surprise. He goes round and round forming something like whipped up cream. He peeks over a railing and down after stepping away from his small bakery. Under the boy at a new level as far as the eye can see white clouds are whirling, until they spin into a perfect pointed top. He turned around and a huge shiny gold container very present is oozing white fluff around the edges. He keeps bending his wrist which is gleaming a soft yellow glow. Surely he did take a big taste from the spoon. Whatever he is eating he seemed to be saying, "yummy." The smile told that about him. A small boy and girl are making their way to the boy with a delivery. Bent over they are trying their very best to keep on pushing a cart over to him, which was carrying a huge three layered white cake. Soft yellow light was coming from thick white candles. The delivery crew wore the tall chef hats. Too cute for words. Chocolate icing was part of the design. Happy Birthday! Right on the top of the cake. Not a wedding cake, but a very big birthday surprise. Why would the kids be praying over cake? Now they tilt their heads with prayer hands softly pressing their face. Pray before you go to sleep.

Feathery gold angels with a solid blue ball of light for a head are unusual, but to dig more into their life should be rather fruitful. Now a pale pink angel with a white crest is balancing a straight flowing gold stick of light on her index finger. We will find out where the other angels are shortly. Her left eye is brown and her right one is blue. It took at least four times to see what she was doing with her eyes, bringing the colors in separately then both at once. A white light very small in size gleams at the top of her gold stick. And why would you think she changed her eye color from just lowering the magic stick forward? Who knows why, but her left eye went from brown to green, but the other remained blue, and her dark pupils had a sparkle.

Back to at least two of the angels with blueness attached to their manifestation. Now just a tiny sliver of blue in the shape of a thread of hair can be seen through both of the lady's thick, long locks of brown hair. They are one. Perhaps the women were preparing to make their inception from behind the rounded blue light which revealed more to whom they were. From inside of a long winding pathway of dark brick every color to heaven's flowers you have ever imagined them to be are beautifully aggrandizing the kingdom of God. A snoopy orange ring tail cat and a very dark brown dog have stopped to smell a yellow and white flower. Why? Because that's what they like to do in the garden. Wild flowers are growing there too, but the red poppies, the tall swaying daisies and yellow pansies are very clean, free from any dirt.

A couple variations of the spirit light came in. Small but very noteworthy. A gold glimmer of eternal light, and there was a baby blue and soft white contact combined. Very far reaching is an enlightening stretch of orange color, but there is something raised up from a launching pad which will be fun to look at. It took off. And that it was a strange rocket ride that skimmed smoothly across the light surface of heaven. At the front was a white whirling sensation of light, and in the rear the same. If it wasn't for the two wings, it would have been thought to be one other ride. It is gigantic in length. All along the outer casing, which is white with black framing around the many windows. Glowing yellow balls of light were bright enough that the people sitting at the windows were aglow. Sometimes the Lord just has to show the inner depths of heaven that way. Even though they traveled quickly on their merry way, the cone shaped front end was seen approaching the opening of a white tunnel. When the ship started coming out from the whirling white light below, and now out in front, it pushed them forward at a tremendous rate of speed. They left in such a hurry that the other white cloud of light was seen turning in motion where the tunnel was. The rocket ship is now erect. It well be explained. They haven't a countdown which they go through for launching. No secret code. The lights on each side are blinking off and on simultaneously. This has got to be good. The passengers and crew are now taking off into new dimensions of exploration. A golden thrust of light sparkles brightly upon the liftoff.

The shining embers of light disappear with a smooth golden light remaining up high. It strengthens though. The rocket ship unexpectedly descends from the light. A boy at the second window encircles his hands, holding them close to his eyes like a pair of binoculars. And the saintly spiritual man in control of the space rocket turns to look from His window. Lo and behold it was Jesus. And the big rocket on its side doesn't drop through the heavens out of control with the Lord present. The Lord is clinching onto a gold cross. He kissed the cross. A pink candle with a yellow flame kindles in the giving spirit of the Lord. It is ever so very soft.

The spirit moves in a movement of stumbling, but in a fast forward motion. Why is the Lord's white robe torn at the knee? He took hold of His garment right between His fingers, where you could even see it come through some. After the Lord removed His entire hand, the garment of our Lord was brand new, mended just by Him rubbing His hand upon it. That will become known of why. The Lord shows in the light, stumbling, and if you really believe in Christ doing miraculous things in the holy spirit, you'll want to accept that He was praying too. So what He meant by His holy message was, when we stumble and fall, all we need to do is call upon Jesus to make everything alright again. Three balls of white light on a forty five degree angle appear with a sharp triangular image for each one of them. They are assembled differently now with two of the images side by side, and the last one, that is the ball of glowing white light with the triangle on top pointing up. The entire middle area is glowing an eternal gold light, if you would for a moment think of them as glowing spiritual lights. Inside the two globes of light below a gold cross is shining. The white glowing sensation on the top, instantly the color changes from a beautiful soft white to baby blue, which is now shedding rays outwardly.

A woman with shoulder length curls of blonde hair is enjoying a stroll inside of heaven, oh so beautiful with a very soft yellow umbrella over her right shoulder. She has a close friend, who's standing right behind her. She has a white umbrella, and her hair is shoulder length, too, but so brown. They're blowing kisses. That is too much to believe, but it's true. If you are alone don't feel bad. They send their love for mankind from their side of life. But they can be seen on our side too. They'll appear, but you need to believe. The gentlemen would like that.

Strong violet light is leading to an opening where white light glows. Standing tall is a dark brown door with a lion's head which is noticeable. Small yellow flowers decorate the arch above the door. The dark brown accentuated the beauty captured much more than our greatest expectations of heaven's spiritual side. Will that door swing open now? The white light has withdrawn some from the opening, but it is still visible around all of the door's edges, including the small walkway of light left out in front of the doorway. The lion head has small sparkling gold eyes that are mysterious. The door has opened up, and wouldn't you like to know what the very first vision became thereto? There stood the Lord, eyes of blue with a contented look upon His face. For fun the Lord took off His gold crown, handling it in a most entertaining fashion indeed. The crown moves downward, and then upward. He repeated doing so for at least ten seconds, and after figuring out that there was white light being sent from the small ball of white light on the very front of His crown, from such an amazing sight happening, thenceforth, multitudes of people in heaven, again, at a lower position, but still equal to the Lord in kinship, reach upward to the Lord. While feeling the penetration of His glorious soothing light all over, inside and outside of their soul they rejoice. It's really wild, but the interpreter can actually see a young man inside of the holy spirit asking the Lord a question about His crown.

The crown was handed to the Lord's child for him to feel, and to circle the crown inside of his hands for his pleasure. The man was in awe, as the pure gold was brightening more and more. What was so clear was the young man giving the Lord back His crown in a hurry, because he knew, the crown really belonged to his Lord and Savior. One thing that automatically happens when the Lord looks directly into your eyes, when He is sitting enormously upon His golden throne, will be a great big smile that comes across your face. How does He do that? If you lost all of the memories of how you felt during your childhood it will all come back in a flash when you see Jesus. You'll be bright-eyed and bushy tailed when you see Him. He has given love.

Heaven isn't all about fancy light rides, but they are still a lot of fun to go on with friends and family. Four people are enjoying one of the rides in the light at a special area. Hands flying up in the air above their heads. The shape of this ride dips inside, almost that being compared to a log flume. A lot of whiteness whirls and rolls around on the outside, and the people come to an abrupt halt. The woman in front looks outside, over the front and downward. Now over to the side and back some. She is very observant. Two boys and a girl sit behind her. An archway of beaming orange light with a gold sparkling light on each side of the entry is entrancing to the group. And they did go inside. Not one but two fast dips through the definable light they're traveling again. The woman in front stopped the ride so her and the riders could watch a whirling white light ride below them, that movement which was controlling a very long black passenger train that was chugging along down the extending railway.

A boy with reddish brown hair was descending from inside of the spirit, guided by his golden wings that pointed outward, while he was seen standing, but slightly resting in a laid back position with the white twirls of light on each side of him. With a gold spark of light coming from the inside corner of his right eye, the boy is all smiles. Now he has landed his ride, and what the boy is wearing will only come as a new study. His robe is silver with gold shiny buttons.

Almost similar to a spacesuit. He's up in the light again, flying now. His arched golden wings stick more upward so they must give him energy to fly inside of the spirit world. At free will.

The fat white candle which just came in a visual was so faint in color you could see through it. Two more candles come hither, soft blue with orange candlelight. Some sort of black entity all curled over with a hunchback tried stealing our thunder, until an angel of God came in and erased it from sight. Just when you thought you were already in heaven living it up with the rest of the festive crowd, that snot had to come along behind God's back. But on the other hand, God may just be testing us a little bit so we'll keep our faith strong in Him and the Lord.

It wasn't a person the angelic spirit removed moments ago. A woman in a nurse's uniform is watching over a baby boy resting inside of a bassinet of white light. And even more special a ball of light begins to spread from the woman's right hand, and that forms a great soft white light upon the babe. She bends over the bassinet even more, revealing her nurse hat. She wants us to learn of the gold cross that gleams on the front of her hat. In other words, she wants us to understand why she is where she is at. She wants everyone to put their fears to rest when it comes to our inner most thoughts about death. She believes with the Lord that we should be worry free, which has been said before inside of the many spiritual messages, expressed by the light workers in one form or another. The nurse was and is a popular person to someone who is enjoying the messages. She helped the ailing before she left earth. There were groups of people around her, and there were several wheel chairs close by, some with people in them and some that were sitting by in case the urgent need came up. The spiritual nurse is happy in heaven right at this moment. She is strolling along in pure white light with the child placed inside of a stroller now. He will enjoy the ride with her assistance.

They'll never be without a beautiful scenery to excite. There is whimsical movement inside of the holy spirit. Many of the Lord's offspring are bouncing about in front of our Lordship. Four children with gold and black striped wings pointing inside out feature the zebra striped effect. The tiny ones are turning slowly, but not into a full circle. Funny as can be each of the angelic children are whispering into the child's ear who stands next to them. Covered in mild yellow light are two girls and two boys. But they are very small. Wouldn't you really enjoy knowing that they're able to enjoy as much laughter and silliness as the rest of us when it comes to having fun? These kids are so adorable that one little boy has bent over at the waist laughing hysterically. And the girl with a full head of dark curls, with her arm around him is checking to see if everything is ok with him. The little angelic boy still covered in the light is pointing to the Lord's white robe, where only His knees and lower part of the garment shows. The Lord told the angelic child something very funny, no doubt, one hundred percent. The Lord enjoys laughter.

Now the sweet angels of God have situated themselves above the Lord, beneath Him, and with an angelic child on each side of the throne. Instead of seeing the striped wings as they were, they've magically changed into only one color, that being bright gold. The Lord rotates a book around inside of His hands, as He has before in the past to share wisdom. But the inside has an almost blinding white light coming from the inside pages. One word is printed across the bright light. It was shown as, "word." Many waxy yellow candles appear now. Exciting to know.

Below the interpreter's feet he can see a very dark mountain on a slanted view. Blue sky is on the side in contour, and a white ball of light is glowing. Partake in a spiritual vision or two of your own. Is the vision similar or the same? You decide that. See how high up in the spirit the Lord can take you? The spirit shows green grass below at the bottom. Two sparkling rivers with silver waves of water, which have been created from spiritual light are in sight. There they are beautiful shade trees with green leaves, even pink and white blossoms have grown upon them. They are flawless. As though the Lord puts a person inside of a deep, captivating spiritual trance that has taken place. A good old fashion out of body experience helps relieve tension, recognized as only that coming from the other side, due to the fact that the interpreter doesn't know how to show visions of which he just went through with the Lord and His viewers.

The spirit wants us to try and go with the flow of the light, respectively. A skywalk of soft white light opened with a heavenly sight. God helps us feel His heavenly generosity by showing us peaceful scenery. Pure white and tan color ferns appear stuck together side by side. But ferns are usually green plant life. But after wondering about them, green ferns begin to sprout up here and there. The other plants which were thought to be intermeshed are beginning to sway slightly back and forth. They even look like patterns of color as many seem planted within the spiritual land of plenty. A huge white hammer appears, but why would the Lord want that in the picture? Believe it or not, He wants us to build with Him. And with the Lord tugging at His own right ear lobe, He makes us feel that He is listening. And He most certainly does have many strange plants. Now dangling strings of golden light hang down from the tan and white plants, and at the bottom secured well were solid gold decorative balls of light. No, it isn't a joke.

The Virgin Mary comes with an infant in Her arms. A very splendid gold light comforts the child. Her being ever so loving to children is a great reminder that She tends to them, not just for short periods, but often it's a duty of Hers. She'll continue doing so as long as the Lord loves them. A huge flame of bright orange fire ensued. But the words, "don't worry" appeared from the Virgin Mary offering us much hope for the best home in heaven. She knows us well. Mary feels that She is a little alarming to some. But She would like you to think of Her as a friend. She is glad you would feel that She is true. Her left hand is offered palm done, soft and gentle Her features are, and with that being said, you'll be pleased to know Mary is wearing a pearl bracelet. Doesn't She deserve to be heard from? She could have been mistaken for a different spiritual vision sent from the other side of life. That isn't so. While offering Her tender hand to us the tip of Her index finger sparkled in gold. But her illustrious silver crown wasn't worn. But She was wearing a very neat white veil over Her head. Have you ever seen the outdoor displays of the Virgin Mary, where She seems to be looking down from heaven? She did appear in a long white robe, and She'll clothe Herself in many ways.

There was one detail left out that just came to mind. Beneath Her veil, some sort of grey layer under cloth was attached to the white covering on Her head. Now the image of Her is extra strong. She is on bended knee inside of a refreshing golden light, praying to our Father above and likely to the Lord for inner strength for the people. She props Her hands against a very large boulder, and to see Mary with closed eyelids and a perfect oval face, praying in the presence of the Lord is absolutely the best Sunday surprise ever, especially for the interpreter who is recording this. Up above inside of the same holy light, Jesus is standing next to a spiritual person with the same length of hair. The blackness covering His friend's face is very mysterious, and that is because, He is secretive. His beard and mustache came through in wholeness of His spirit.

A person in a bright vanilla light, just as he is standing so close to a blackboard with chalk in one hand, unbelievably, he is ready to write something out. He wrote, "Love Your Neighbor." The real magic was that the thinker walked away so quickly, and even though we would have expected small words to be placed in front of us to read, they came out about twelve inches high.

A whirling white light ride has accelerated again inside heaven. More of a huge shining golden cone of light below the whiteness is spotlighted. Very glorious and awakening.

Not your usual everyday pure blue clouds made up the backdrop. Instructed in the light to be disclosed. A blue cloud cover on the left is discharging the soft golden flowing light beneath the next ride. All has lifted up. The twist inside of the light proves the whirling white light ride has been moving about. Then an image appears again. A gold cross shines upon the glorious marvel. If this wasn't told you wouldn't realize that the Lord has something to say through His little helper. As the whirling light turns gradually in clockwise motion, two imprints of angel wings appear against the white light. The wings, however, feathery and lightly colored in gold speak for themselves. But who is this? A good side view of a lady appears between the wings with appealing long golden hair with undeniable, gorgeous brown eyes. She is wearing a gold crown with silver sparkling diamonds. Not a King's royal crown, but holy looking enough still. Her pursing lips brings out the dimple on her cheek. She says, using wording in the light, "You could call it a ride if you want." She might make you shake your head in disbelief still, but with more of a positive spin inside of this pleasant ordeal with our angelical friend.

A white cross turned sideways with glowing mint green balls of light, across from each other at two ends, seemed interesting in the spirit. The angelical woman presses the image against her white robe glowing with imprinted yellow flowers. She rests the cross upon her soft shoulder, while she looks downward somewhere in the heavens, only to surprise us with her cross creating mint green skies above her now. Where she is at taking the ride of her life, she held out the cross in front of her own spirit, watching a creative smooth white light travel far from the edge of the cross. At its destiny the stream of light created, yet, another whirling white sensation.

A dark gazebo appeared, and a cloudy white light was now located behind the interesting structure. The light behind our King makes Him and everyone else up in heaven that much more stronger. Even the faith our Lord has in His Father and Mother in helping everyone is plentiful. Suddenly, several triangle flag shape, white lights fill in the area of the empty gazebo. Then all of a sudden the lady points her white cross to the gazebo, and the entire structure turned gold. The upper part sparkled more. You know what? The gazebo looks like a gigantic bird cage. For an important reason, the Lord has us now looking down at the golden gazebo in a higher dimension. The angel has traveled up high in spirit.

She points her cross down to the gazebo creating white clouds around the Lord's property. The golden light beneath her is spreading, but the shade is much milder. She is slowly releasing the darling little white angels, forthwith, going into the spirit world to fly and adventure freely. Inside of the rest of the golden light a large gold star appears bursting in color. She brings the fancy gazebo to eye level now, straight across from where she admires it.

As far as one can tell the angelic woman is being straightforward, about her herself and the visions from God. Now that we have a pretty good idea of who has been guiding us in a harmless manner, we will use some more time up on our side to see where she is heading, and to figure out who she is approaching. Her golden crown becomes more brilliant to see. Wow! Decorous as such as to where it comes to an appreciable rounded edge on top, as the front has slanted gold, some which swirls to the top of her head. A white angel wing is arching away from her, as its rounded head is almost at knee level. Therefore the angel with the golden light, which was covering her face and hair, stands inside of her white light from her midriff down to greet the angelical friend. Sure enough, while admiring the beautiful robe of yellow flowers, that woman reaches down to the white angel, and straightens out both wings, and they are spread across the guest so graciously now. The angelic guardian speaks in the holy spirit, but even though she wasn't heard, her mouth opened when turning away looking into the heavens. A yellow lily appeared near her face in mid-heaven. Perhaps she softly spoke the beautiful flower into life. Being hesitant and wise is good.

In the spirit, there's a two-tone heart, the left side is black and the right area is red. The heart is upright and sits upon dark blue velvet. A string of pearls was just hung across the heart, and truthfully, the interpreter was surprised to see that. It was very hard telling where they were going with the heart. You would think that a bust of the Virgin Mary just appeared on the right side, and the Lord over to the left side of the heart, but they came in such soft white light, that's what had transpired. Without being frightened by this, Mary opened Her hand to show She was holding a small gold cross, and there was a curl of pearls too. A clinched fist pulls up on a single thin string, where a box opens up releasing three balloons. One was yellow and the other two were white, starting to lift up into the spirit. Three children in soft white and yellow light, combined, received the floating balloons from the Lord who is very presenting. The Lord reminds us in the light to believe in the interpretations. The kids with the balloons were happier about their gifts received. They like to release the balloons and watch them fly around in heaven. A little boy with the darkest shoulder length hair covering his ears runs forward, faster and faster until he picks up enough speed to let his yellow balloon take off from his hand.

There has to be a special purpose behind his balloon reaching someone inside the heavens, because he is at a standstill, praying with his hands pressed firmly together. He could be trying to tell us to be giving through prayer. Hold on, he is twisting both of his hands around. Through the Lord, the boy opens his hands and holds them up to see. They were very clean. In fact, so very pure that there was glowing white light coming from the inside. Face forward it is much easier to see the boy's chestnut brown eyes. The clarity and depth within his eyes is amazing. And he has a thick and neat hair bang.

The spirit world has so much to offer, even if it was just the spiritual blue sky way up here, and the puffy white clouds nearby now. That's how high up the conscious mind has been raised during these precious moments. We already know our thoughts have reached higher up into heaven above. A black outlined synagogue window appears with a high arch. On the other side of it there eternal light turned a beautiful soft blue. Suddenly a huge depth of yellow light covers the entire window, leaving the black outline of its structure less defined. Soon three other arch shaped windows fill in all around the first. There's an open square of them glowing in this soft yellow light. Not being a total expert on the spirit world, but close enough as a learner of divinity through the spiritual gift of discernment, a small gold cross appeared inside of each window in the center of the tall, but very thin black cross, which was part of the inner structure. The gold crosses may be small, but they are very powerful, shedding light onto the world through much darkness. They glow a lot and are very sensational.

A very innocent child in a mild golden light stands knee high to a grasshopper, but in this case, he is surrounded by a crowd of religious people on his left, and the Lord is definitely on his right, where the child is looking to Him for guidance. And if the men and women who seem to be standing up higher than the child on a wide balcony, but yet still very much within his company are not "religious" then they're very spiritual, due to being up here in the heavens. Everyone is covered in the golden light still, a good feeling is coming from their side, where strong encouragement comes to love one another. It's hard to hate up here in the light, the Lord's heart, mind and His soul is that of love. The grownups kind of remind you of gods and goddesses, but the Lord knows better, there is only one God, His divine Father. It must be the holy look about them then. The child's entire head and face has been covered by two hands. After debating what is right and what may be wrong to say, the Lord prefers to go on with the interpretation.

He even appears behind the child, and as the Lord stands there, they've both closed their eyes and are in heavenly prayer. Jesus and the boy temporarily step outside of the golden light which covered them. The child and Jesus wore white robes. There stood Jesus, blue eyes sparkling again. The people watching are very entertained by prayer and healing from laying on of the hands, so inspirited by the Lord that they're clapping their hands and smiling, convinced the Lord is a healer. What the heck. This is the vision, really. One penny, two penny, three penny, four, with the golden light shining from the tunnel ahead, just look inside and you'll see more. The Lord believes in us that much, if we seek out that glowing light straight ahead, from where we are, concentrating on the afterlife will bring us into a fantastic creation of sheer delight.

Out into the distance a whirling white light has stemmed from the fascinating golden tunnel. A young woman wearing a tall black hat with a white feather comes marching in with a small band behind her. A few others wear dark uniforms, as does she, but what's so unique about these heavenly people is that with each movement, they bow quickly. The leader's right hand is bright white now. She has touched the whirling light. Her left hand holds a black and white swirling wand, which she now reaches out to touch the mass of white curling light. But within a few short moments later, five people are covered with the light, and they have not only taken a bow, but they have curved backs and are down on all four. Above the curls and whirling light on top of the entertainers, there's a small orange flame.

The leader with the tall hat is in a more milder white light now. She leans in to blow out the flame. But as she did do that, her face was revealed, clearer, meaning a good look into our world. Hopefully that long brown hair of hers will become a little looser around the chin strap. She just let it hang where ever she chose to. Not that she was uncomfortable with herself, it was funny to see someone with so much hair everywhere. The backside of their dark uniforms were seen. They marched away in weaving movement. The figure of the woman leading, took a second to bow forward a wee bit with her hat in her hand, and she winked. Her eyes are brown.

Some things in heaven will really tickle your funny bone. An impressionable delicate ray of soft white light from above provides a nice circle of light for the fellow below. He seems so tiny, just his black top hat could be seen, besides the light becoming much brighter where he stood at the center of attention. As he tipped his hat then his face was visible, but as far away as he is it was an effort noticing him, if it wasn't for the hat. Even with the significance of hats lately, they're doing a magnificent job of keeping us entertained. He was about to throw his hat up into the heavens. But he just wanted to salute his Maker, who was the Lord, who is now covered with a sparkling gold halo. With the Lord being so close in attendance we'll never have a problem. The entertainer down in the spotlight pulled a rabbit out from another hat. Right by his ears. Can he do that in heaven, and is that cruelty to animals? Apparently not a harmful act. But a brilliant gold castle appears in the same spotlight as the man and his furry white friend with inner pink ears. Puffy white letters stretch across a very wide black cloud. The word was "celebrate." For the sake of being helpful to the Lord, He showed a luger suspended in the spirit, and a touch of soft blue light glowed between the trigger and handle. Guns do kill people, and it doesn't take a mathematician to figure that out. Into the light people go. A bare chested man is holding onto whirling light as though he was riding inside of an inner tube. The word "shot" in black lettering was shown. He knows it's perfect where he is now. He gives the "ok" signal with his fingers. As for the super fantastic light ride it is an enjoyable feeling. He thought that he was in a dream at first. A man who is the shop owner or a bread maker has fallen to his knees. His large white apron is being folded by someone in the light. With large loaves of bread, unwrapped, they were sitting in the man's shop inside a glass counter, much like pastries are.

Out of respect for the man a white robe has been given to him to wear. And he is weeping in the Lord's hands. The shopkeeper is holding his throat. The earth in global form, and the white tunnel were now presented. The man pointed to earth. He had throat problems, whereas he couldn't breath when suffering from a heart attack. What to expect. His white robe has a nice smooth tail. It's very soft, and as he rises in heaven with eyes gazing upward, even though three balls of white light are whirling all around him, the inner spin to them is slow with a feathery whiter path leading him away to where he finds placidity. Think of it as a journey into the spirit with friends when you arrive. Better yet, we'll let you decide what is what, and who is who in heaven. But a lot of people will need a guide to help along the way with evolving.

A nice full gold cloud has settled inside of the holy spirit. Also, we shall hear about the two children sitting on top of white mounds across from one another. Somehow they've become attached to the lining of the large golden cloud. The boy up on the right and the girl are holding onto red and white striped candies. Is this coming from daydreaming, or would this be from a higher conscious contact with

God? The light is powerful. We will go with that thought, and if you thought it was sent from heaven, you would probably be right.

A gold star shines. Yes it was a reappearance in the light. Off on the side where there is a noticeable walkway with white light, a man with golden hair is about all ready to send over to the children, angels, and although they're very pretty, some sort of mysterious silver glowing light coming from their necks is radiating a huge background of color behind the children. The angels have faces which are sparkling in gold, though. The children have touched down deeper inside of the gold cloud. They are very comfortable inside of it with them watching from small windows. But in a flash, the gold cloud turns into a gigantic disc of white light that is endlessly held together by the light of goodness and of God. The spirit boy and girl are whispering into the angel's ears. The ears can't be seen, but the children were leaning forward with their hands held close to them. Think of them as real. White chairs appear on the inner surface, where the angels and the children are. They're in their seats now. That's right, one was provided for everyone. The angels are people too. The kids have rounded their arms way out, and brought back around, moving them so we understand that they're about to start turning slowly. Truthfully, they are real sitting in white robes.

The one golden face angel looks over to the girl. The back of the boy's auburn hair shows us they have begun to whirl a little bit more. The other angelic friend is near. Wait! The surface of white light that is turning is starting to rise up from below. They can't be shut out from our life. One of the angels with golden hair all of a sudden has a dark beard. How could that be? He opens his mouth while seeming to whirl upward in a slow motion. With big white teeth a silver spark shines in his mouth. All four are still sitting on this rising surface of the whirling white light. The angels and the kids have grown so big. While they're having all the fun, we have to sit back and think about praying to the Lord and Father God again. Why is that so? How else will we be able to experience the sensation of the ride that's fully maximized in the light?

Secondly, slanted prayer hands are offered in a "light" vision. Two huge white clouds and stirring motion have prompted an easy interpretation. Let the Lord take you out from your body through the "whirling" ride prayer request. If we try to believe in this grand experience it will come. It should become a nightly prayer request. It's going to blow your mind, and your grandparents would enjoy the trip back and forth from heaven too. They may just be ahead of our time in the light if already there. The exact green light that we see outdoors on the street corner is bright. The leaning telephone pole with only that certain light, which was at the opposite end, on top, was to get our attention. It's a sign from the afterlife.

A very large bird cage is hanging from a gold hook. Inside a small yellow finch is tweeting. You know something? As it was being described the tiny tweet was heard. Makes you squint your eyes, almost in disbelief. But with this many spiritual experiences, we just keep on believing in that wonder working power of the lamb. The cage door swung open. The birdie rests upon someone's flat hand. With a white sleeve showing from the robe worn by the possessor of the bird, He lets her fly over on in through the divine white light. If you have keen enough intuitiveness, you'll see the canary over on an approximate forty five degree angle from where you sit. The bird is perched on a brownish, small branch or stick. Cutely, she rests in the divine.

A mysterious archer aiming a tipped arrow high is in the darkness, but very near the light of God. The large bow now points away from the high heavens, and slants down to the ground in a restful motion. The dark figure has become filled with the holy spirit now. His angel has white wings. Sparkling gold specs of light have clung to the soft angelic archer. Inside of the light the bow and arrow turned solid white and has been tipped upside down. As a reward the angelic soul was given a big u-shaped harp. It does change from solid gold back to white again. A very nice gift indeed. Just when you thought the angel from the dark would most likely be turning against God and His people, the Lord has contributed another fine example of how He has forgiven His enemies. Do you feel God's little helper was officially anointed?

That canary resting upon her perch looks very peaceful still. It couldn't be helped to wonder if the archer was aiming the arrow at her. Why should the word "tweet" appear in black lettering after all of that? Perhaps she is more aware of us than we thought she'd be.

The spirit begins to shift away from the earthly level, where the messages come to, and then wait, spiritual activity begins again. You'd be surprised how the Lord holds His attention on the heavens and on our side too. The Lord's shoulders are in view, the white robe covering them. He tends to be watching over His shoulder observing us. He said something. A white puffy light came from out of His mouth, while it was sensed that He spoke one word during the release.

The holy spirit wants everyone to believe that whether it was your parents and grandparents first, fifth, tenth, twentieth, thirtieth, fortieth, or even fiftieth and later in years, celebration of your wedding anniversary, you'll still be able to celebrate your memories in heaven with your beloved. With the bride in her wedding gown, and the groom wearing his tails in the spirit sharing wedding cake, there's no doubt that you'll feel good, but expect to look and experience your youthful state of mind and higher self within the state of well-being. The spirit is showing a fifty in numeral form, and the word "anniversary" on a wedding cake. The couple, surprisingly, they would be guessed to be in their twenties, but they're still celebrating fifty years of happy marriage. Even if it sounds funny, the spiritual vision here in the heavens is trying to help you realize the relationship to marriage, between you and your spouse, once you've reached their side. The couple enjoying the wedding cake are happy about their youthful side.

Who would have thought you'd be watching children and adults parachuting inside of the mystical heavens of endless beauty, without the use of any lines? One pearly white angel was with them, but there must be other groups of people and angels doing the same. There is a woman and a man looking downward with their head hanging, while raising their hands up to where the lines should be to guide them. With the powers in heaven, they are guided with white whirling light shaped as chutes, which have a bright shining gold light preoccupying the background. Now the power of the golden light makes the white whirls solid gold, but it drizzles some of the coloration down behind all three, which now includes the angel. With a better idea of what's happening, the golden drizzle formed makeshift lines, about four behind everyone. But the inner spiritual power to command such movement of the whirling white to descend within such a holy light is mighty. With their angel friend, they can all count their blessings. The suggestions are that they have such a good God, giving of Himself in the light, that He and the kindness and love felt inside of the light, hugely, follows us through eternity.

How very interesting, the black telescope aimed right toward the white foggy light. Is it really that hard to see through the light? We don't need binoculars or a telescope to look for the other side of life to arrive. Focus is the key. Hear the "spiritual" word, then look for the scenery if you wish to do so. The Lord is very tall right now. Especially a feeling of peace comes just from seeing His soft robe, knowing the Lord stands near, where no germs or disease lives inside of our spirit with Him afterwards. That should be now too. But He gives hope. Not to sound repetitious, but the Lord has a solid white ball of light on His far left, while standing sideways, and the planet earth is formed in front of Him. He doesn't want His message forgotten, as He has stretched up into the white light, and then down to our side, He mentions "healing" again. In the creation of heaven of pure soft golden light comes a woman down on her knees with her face resting closely near His feet. Two spirit filled hands belonging to Jesus have touched her gently upon both sides of her face. A gold star shines above her head and one by the Lord's right foot now. Wow! In the light the interpreter just saw the saying, "Faith Of A Mustard Seed." The Lord is bold.

Special bouquets of very colorful flowers are being set upon large white table blocks. There is a tender child in a yellow dress with a with a white bow and flowers at her waistline. She is walking quickly in the spirit with the deliveries. Thought to be key chains attached to the bouquet was incorrect. They have name tags attached which are hanging from the side. There are people's names on them. Some of the flowers have thick sparkling gold bows and some are thinner. They mention requests by guides to visit special areas. Now there's a pleasant surprise. You have to love the Lord. He comes to the rescue again. He is bending forward with a bouquet of flowers in His hands. You'd think He was at a wedding walking down the isle, He is so gentlemanly. The tag on the flower arrangement has black lettering. It says, "Just For You." The flowers are red, green, yellow and white. A single yellow rose lay limp on a table, until a small amount of white light touched the petals to make it stand straight, bringing an unusual sight.

These invisible spirits would be enough to give you the willies if you didn't understand they come from the spirit world made by God. A giant of a brunette woman with long curls down past her shoulders came and went. She wore a smokey white robe. Thought to have left and never to return, She is back now. She has a white bow on the left side of Her hair, thought to be girlish. You know that surprised look you'd get if you won the lottery? She has a peanut shaped mouth, larger and more expressive than you'd expect. There are four cotton like clouds beneath Her, and what a surprise. She is sitting on a solid gold throne, back up in the heavens.

They inform the female presence is here, because our Father God's image will change without notice. She is flaunting a diamond bubble ring. Probably the only one like it in heaven with a silver band. She is showing that is has an inner gold glow which sparkles above the diamonds, something not even noticed beforehand. Why did She just twist Her hair and lean? She also turned a long silver fish into gold color. It could have been Her light taking control. She has the power of an incredible God or Divine being.

Many small lambs are grazing, not in an ordinary field, but one that has tall yellow flowers and swaying wheat from a very gentle breeze. But for the lambs, the nourishment they receive comes from a magical golden light that is richly poured out from an ordinary bucket. The light is gleaming brighter. With the lambs being saturated with light, the two farmers in dark bib overalls, who have been tipping the buckets in front of them, fed the group, and somehow to where each lamb understood that the eternal light was wonderful to see and feel. And obviously even good enough to taste. Mouths moving side to side tell the truth. The farmers in heaven are kind. Best to know about the nature of farmers, how they look and feel much the same inside.

Smooth and loving with the holy spirit. The images God and the Lord have are visual. It is almost hilarious. The angel God has actually slides across the landscape of heaven. Very much an interesting move. But the angel is very thin, outlined in black, one wing which has raised a circular ball of white light with a dark outer ring. The halo to our visitor in the spirit remains white for right now. The same outer appearance, as the study upon the tip of its wing up in the air excites. The angel's robe is black and white with that inward hook shape. Something to absorb mentally and spiritually. This was nice. The angel without revealing eyes bowed down before a gold stream, dipped the circular ring of light inside and scooped out eternal freshness.

A pale blue candle which is rather tall stands behind the growing angel. That candle was created in the shape of a number one. Above the special candle a small white flame appeared. Golden rays of brilliant light spread wider and wider, which have been created from transcendental streams. As the black ringed, white ball of light changes into solid gold from a tremendous overlay, the angelic presence bows down and brings the sparkling halo to place it as a topping. Known as a refreshed halo now. The angel's face comes in view, although it looks almost mummified. Even a white flesh appearance, but in heaven the angel's face is of the spirit.

There is room to celebrate. Near the growing angel, two angelic friends are present. With wings spread out like a flying eagle a solid blue angel is jubilant. A white angel on the right has an announcement to make. That comes by way of the white horn similar to a megaphone, which is spoken through. At the edge of the tip to the horn a more brighter white line of light glows from the inside presenting a sudden burst of more white lines. Better told than concealed. They're celebrating their friend's spiritual experience with the new golden halo. Now that the Lord reveals more, the angel's once "mummied" face has changed to a very clear complection, and that of a woman with gigantic yellow butterfly wings. A huge bunch of white carnations are held inside of her hands, and she offers them. One by one, four of the flowers were interspersed into the heavens, yet very close to her and the angels who celebrate in a silly way.

There are many red and white thin striped, robed angels about now. Not just their garments, but the halos are striped, and tilting topsy-turvy. They have cute little feet, not expecting to see them so up close like that the adorable kids have sparkling gold sticks in their hands. An image to take to one's grave, if you believe in angels. Little white flowers are worn across some of their bare feet in a dainty group of three, and some of the angelic children appear to have crisscross dark sandals on. Cutely, the many peppermint striped angels choreograph themselves about in the design of one very big red and white design of an angel. Red bows are their's to wear.

And the glittering gold in heaven never ceases to amaze. Two solid gold angels about ten inches high, flip over showing off more gold on the bottom to each. And then one gold candlestick beneath both appeared. They were identical to materialistic items and would be very valuable to people on earth. In the spirit, though, you'll find colorful light on everything and everyone. A dark haired boy has a few raisins in the palm of his hand. While we still ponder the question on eating fruits in heaven, that's a given for sure. The kid is a ghost. He won't mind us accepting him like that. First he held four spread out fingers in front of his mouth, before squatting with both hands then resting upon his knee caps. He read the interpreter's thoughts and mind as well. Heaven even has all knowledge of us before we think.

Much activity of the whirling white light ride in heaven begins at the bottom, with yet another mass, where a wide gap is evident with the cloud in the higher element. Pretty secure on the inside, and appearing on the side of the whirl, leaning out, a boy and a girl are wearing gold pointed party hats upon their head. As they peek out from the inner whirling of white light, they are tooting, and swirling gold and silver decorated party horns which they enjoy. With some change they are pretty much inside of a mild golden light, too, inside the lower area where they're snug as a bug in the clouded ride. There isn't a need to walk if they don't need to. The boy over on the left side, he even wonders to himself what should be said now. With a small string tied around his index finger, he bounced his arm around in the direction of the girl still hanging out from the other side in a sweet way.

A white spec of light was seen inside of her dark brown eyes. She sees in the light is the best explanation for the unusual discovery. She hugs the white whirl like she is in love with it. Like looking at huge masses of white cotton candy. There's some motion happening, which is suggestive of the children going for a ride. But why is there another huge white whirling light heap in the middle? In deep mediation we shall find out the answer shortly. The Christ light above the children flattens out across the top of the gigantic white mass. Two tall red velvet chairs with a small gold cross at the top are what the two children will sit upon now. The next image came in faster than usual. Both of the kids have felt their way into the very comfortable seating arrangement, and they have placed their arms on the golden armrests.

The blue sky is miraculous. Hot air balloons are up high and low with riders viewing the children down below. The whirling white light has begun to lift from the center, bringing the entire ride together. The children are sitting side by side viewing keyboards. They are inputting something that instantly created three silver stars around the ride. There isn't a rocker to fall off, the kids are sharing the mysteries of heaven. It's a new way of having church with us, you could say. There's a wide perimeter around the Lord. It's made up of the same whirling white light ride, and without your reading glasses, that is so highly noticeable. Don't feel sorry if you don't see them when you attempt to. The words in visible gold light is evidence. They say, "I Would Like To Share The Ride With You." Expect a little more to happen when you believe in prayer. Won't you wait on the Lord to lift you up into the light? Ask for the uplifting ride.

A huge group of people from firemen, real Indians with feathers, the Dutch along side of black, white, and Asian children, have come together as enormous crowds of other lineages were presently welcome nearby. A fireman wearing a black helmet stretches a glowing white light out between his hands and forms a whirl of white light, that has brought some to tears and some women are so grateful, they smile happily. They're pressing hands against their cheeks with eyes opened wider than your own. The very prominent white feathered Indian is serving up a puffed blue, and even a much softer layer of blue light, holding his hand up high, palm facing the heavens. He is what you'd expect in a waiter, at least when you're in heaven to enjoy his service. He has caused a little bit of laughter. A little Indian boy with that black and white feather in his headband has hastily thrown a small white dart of an arrow, that has bushy red feathers, through the air it went, landing on the elder's hand of eternal blueness.

The elder, unaware of it coming, which was a surprise, looks puzzled. And that's saying a lot for someone who is very cognizant in the spirit world of spirituality. The feathery arrow was laying flat. The Dutch woman standing near to the entertainers of heaven, bows down with blue and yellow flowers in her hand. Children walk up to her, and out of humanitarianism the girls had one flower of their choice, and it was placed in their hair. The woman with the long white dress embroidered with dark fringe, and a large black front pocket, continued to move her hands in and out for the little ones to choose which flower was best for them to keep. If you could see the boy with the beautiful yellow flower, he held it close to his nose and anyone could tell he was in sweet heaven now. That was very nice of Jesus to help us know these people, and his dear little angels who have life, considerably. What shall the Lord do for us next?

Two ivory white angels a distance across from each other are pondering the same question. Why is that true? The angels are boys, told by their features. They have just been graced with a tinge of gold across their faces, but they remain curious with each angelical boy still thinking about what was upcoming soon. They're deep thinkers, and their little index fingers are going to make a tiny crease in their chins if they keep them there much longer. The darlings were what was next on the agenda, and you could bet, they didn't even know that they were. Such peace in heaven with these two guys. Really soft green color, three prong leaves sit beneath these two angels where a lot of heavenly white light is glowing in the background.

Two huge white cakes, one in back of the other. But is that nothing more than a reflection in a river of the first cake? One candle is present, and an orange flame. The holy spirit is celebrating our birthday in heaven, the same birth date, which is the exact day that we are rejoicing with family and friends. And they are pleased that you should take note. Two large white gift wrapped packages with black ribbon around them await you in heaven. Visible now, yes they are, on each side of the Lord's feet, up there in plain view. Where His white robe drapes forward from His knees on down to His feet, soft glowing white light is displaying the gifts.

While waiting here on the Lord to present more of the fantastic family events in heaven, noticeably, He appears in the spirit world holding a gentle hand close to His ear, as to be listening for a prayer to come. Sometimes the interpreter needs more help than he would like to admit. Two boxing gloves come in the light, but for what reason? Don't fight it and the messages will come. The Lord tells the interpreter, through spirit communication, the audience will wonder if the whirling white light ride in heaven is authentic enough. Truly the best ever ride you'll enjoy in your entire life. Think of it as a daydream if you will. Or a super colossal dream that comes true when you are fast asleep.

If you're having a small problem drawing in the light at night for the "experience" try to meditate with the holy spirit. Resting flat on your back start drawing in white flourishing eternal light through the bottom of your feet, while closing both eyes. It may seem invented in a sense, because of the many thoughts that are in your mind, but never forget that the holy spirit comes in all shapes, sizes, and of color. The spirit is demonstrating something new. Believe that the white is a sharp stripe of light, shaded with a little pink to its edge. There is a level in the spirit world where it began. Even though the pink vibration of light seems stronger in the higher elevation of heaven, comprehend the whiteness beginning to shine between your feet, spreading beautiful white light. Both feet should be covered in the "Christ" light.

The white light has resumed to move about, from the bottom of your feet to the very top of your head. This way your mind will become more attune with the holy spirit. As God's children, we're allowed to draw in the positive light from the other side of life. You'll very much be in touch with the Lord and Almighty God then, which ultimately puts you in the spotlight. It will be fifty-fifty, whether or not that you'll begin seeing the white light traveling around inside of your body, or within your mind and soul, when you're deep in a meditative state with eyes closed in stillness. In darkness anyone can watch the white flowing upward, but it may be less bright than with eyes closed. Nevertheless, God's white light may travel at lightening speed, surprising you. Experiment by whirling the white light up to the crown of your head. If you enjoy the light movement, keep concentrating into the center of darkness as you would when sleeping at night. Draw the white light from the tunnel and nourish yourself with God's everlasting holiness. Don't worry about returning to your body once God has begun lifting you. That's what the whirling white light is all about, pleasure inside of the heavenly kingdom of our Lord. No demons or monsters will ever interfere. The Lord's prayer hands are hugging the white tunnel of light right now. He shall give unto you the spiritual ride, blessings and good tidings galore.

If one should become stumped how to bring the light in bright, think of a winding staircase of whiteness, curling and swirling from the bottoms of your soul. The choice is yours. Eyes open or eyes closed. One hundred percent of the time, you'll depart from the earthly world, deeper into the heavenly light we will go with eyes remaining unopened. Just ask to see the heavens. God will give you a gold star for you attempting to reach Him. Perhaps you'll keep your thoughts to yourself after the lift. What is rather keen to the eye is the holy spirit giving more of the demonstration which He feels will become part of the outcome through our meditation study, for extreme out of body sightseeing. She is a woman with shoulder length hair laying flat in her bed. White light covered her well. Her soul is lifting. But she has stopped moving, the visual of her unfolds, as though she had raised herself up in a recliner, and then after hesitation, she begins moving again inside of the spirit. Three exact images of her were in view.

Not a few white bowling pins or bottles covered in white light, but an actual human being from our side has been used as a valuable example. If there was anyone having an out of body experience at this time in life it would have been her, with the utmost attention, factually. Many of the out of body experiences result in God's children sitting or standing up inside of the light. But as we have been told, the spiritual children and adults in heaven do rest in several positions. The woman helped into the spirit has drawn our attention because of the multiple movements from inside of her restful sleep state, to an awakening, that which the Lord and God is determined to have us believe in as an important finding. The meditation will work with help too.

There isn't anyone on God's green earth who can tell you that the whirling white light ride will give you vertigo. Glory is still a luxury which can be afforded to the non-believers. The passage into heaven is beautiful. The woman inside of bright white seems to be returning to her body. The spirit brings her back down to where she resides in two greater and very soft movements. Funny how the Lord reveals her face now. She is laying flat on her back in a very peaceful frame of mind. Our lovely is facing heaven. A wonderful white light has spread across her midriff, undoubtedly from the holy spirit with that dainty yellow flower given.

A curtain, very soft and white made from whirling white light has formed an arch above a throne. The cloudy whiteness has fallen beneath that royal seat. It's clustered together nicely, seemingly not going anywhere. The beautiful Virgin Mary's face appeared. She looks downward from Her high seat of supreme authority. Don't be worried, She is loving and forgiving. Her hands nearly touch together. She is so peaceful. Her head tilted some, She is feeling well in heaven, a saint by all means, the truest sight of the Virgin Mary, likely the peace She feels inside will be in store for all who enter heaven to be with Her. Her robe color has changed. Now grey and red softness. Many angels surround Her. She speaks in the spirit. "For a moment," She says. The visual experience is very spiritual. The holy angels have come carrying music instruments. A trombone is present, a violin and some horns. One instrument held closely for tapping out sweet sounds would surprise many.

Not quite a dozen angels surround Her for the moment, but She has the right to pick and choose how many people are presently before Her, angels included. We don't want Her to leave now. She said, "Thank you." Your choice to believe Her. The words were seen inside of Her holy spirit in black letters. Her moments may be forever and a day. Her generosity exceeds the norm, and we are all about to visit with Her more if we can. There are angels beneath Her throne, lightly pressing up against the whirling white light that is still there at the base of Her seating arrangement. Gradually the angels rotate around Mary, happily, and they rejoice in Her name and lovely presence. She desires we think pleasant thoughts. Some of us have been chosen to carry the message. Thankfully the holy spirit will touch you today, mentally, physically and inside of your heart and soul to relax your nerves more. You know that She loves you too. Feel Her presence. Her healing touch was just felt by the interpreter. Even if She doesn't remove any infirmities right at this moment, knowing that She can use Her holy spirit and infinite power to touch you inside and outside of your body, as that should be enough to rely on with Her. Was that ever relaxing what Mary did. She'll acknowledge the children of the Lord, even if our memory doesn't serve us well at times. The amazing eternal blue heavens behind Her is jaw dropping.

The white cloud mass beneath the throne has suddenly taken a different turn of events, but hard saying if it was done on its own, or if Mary and the angels had something to say about the unusual enlargement. Why is that happening? The whirling massive light formation has covered Her angels, leaving imprints of them on the inside blanket. The light whirls quite smoothly at that, not into a cone shape, but much wider still. Rolls of white light continue to rise up above Mary's bosom. Her face is still visible. Gladly, Her moment in heaven has lasted for some time down here now. She enjoys light. It's forever filled with the love of Christ.

When asking God in prayer about what was next to be shown, He said, using visible wording, "My Son will guide you." Pretty neat having our heavenly Father relate messages, whether they were short or long ones it is the whole conception that He has done so, even when most people believe that it's fundamentally impossible to do so at the drop of a hat. Seeking out the Lord is easy. A huge white cloud, which seems to be at a distance of about a mile away inside of the holy spirit has covered a mountain with its glorious spiritual light now. But the high mountain has been highlighted with blue light, combined with the whiteness, so wonderfully that the peak glows similar to a frosted shade. The change was fast but beautiful. Perhaps Mary allowed the mountain to change in color at will. She loves the many blues of the holy spirit.

The Shepherd's cane is standing still in the white light which is flowing in waves past it presently. His cane is ivory white. The light has consumed much inside of the holy spirit, except for the Lord's hand. He has a very firm grasp around the cane now. Perhaps it is a gentle breeze or the soft ruffle from the Lord's white sleeve which left the impression that it was moving. Unless between the moments that Jesus moved quickly to fetch the cane, His robe moved more. There is calm in the spirit as Christ stands back a little. The expression He is giving out is of deepest regard, yet, His mouth has opened in surprise of the big flock tree. He stands before the masterpiece in the light. The tree was instantly created from scratch. About in the middle of the tree, although nearer to the front left section, a very beautiful sparkling silvery gold Christmas ball has been decorated with an image of the Lord's church on the ornament.

You can see an amazing cross that's radiating a golden light. The Lord takes hold of the ornament, and He looks upon His creation, even though it is only a Christmas decoration it has significant meaning for one and for all. Likely, the woman leaning over to Christ in a soft and very golden light is Mary, and Her Son hands the ornament over to Her, which turned to pure gold with a million tiny sparkles. The white flock tree seemed to fade away, except for two rows of branches. While observing closely on the other side of life, it's now appreciable that they weren't full branches from the tree, they're ruffled angel wings. For the male angle, he comes with a white halo, and his lady angel friend's was beaming gold. The couple is doing a bit of a tangle dance. Back and forth, they strut their stuff in compatible movement together. Their robes, white as can be, look very stunning with gold buttons that have an inner bronze design against small swirling indentations. Now there is much more emphasis on them holding their hands together. Just seeing their firm hold suggests unity and forever loving each other. It may or may not be hard understanding why they send this message to you. Wording comes from them, by using black letters to form a sentence. "We are proud of you." We don't fully understand why they would say such a thing, but from what we have learned from the Lord we are to love everyone and everybody. Still it's nice to know someone cares from above.

A sleek golden curved shape lamp appears like magic up inside of the majestical heaven. Then, folded prayer hands. Nothing else, but white foggy light is in the picture. That's what we feel prayer is like, rubbing a magic lamp for our wishes and dreams to come true. The Lord thinks you deserve the best is why He brings these images before you to think over. Lift up His name and you shall be rewarded. A small puffy gold cloud of penetrating light, magically effuses from the lamp with a gold cross appearing. It doesn't matter how often the Lord's holy cross is presented, it's our's to keep. Suddenly the lamp turns pitch black. Three puffy black clouds shoot out from the tip, which was wild. What happed to our dreams and wishes not being fulfilled and all we end up with is a sunken feeling of heartache and despair? The Lord feels we need to look at our feelings closer, because if we take into consideration the visual representations the Lord offers us in the spirit to our advantage, we'll see how our emotions can change without bringing along any damaged goods. Go from the old to the new. When our days are cloudy and grey, instead of feeling like we were still left out in the dark, we should pray, because the Lord has told us, from now on, our prayers to Him will be highly appreciated. The Lord is here inside a perfect white door of light, regally sitting upon His throne. He watches over you, and you know He does, because He is peacefully looking down from His throne in heaven. Christ is there with you.

Please let Him hold your hand and try to heal you. Ask Him to. Why do you think the Lord keeps coming in the light? He has work to do. Take time right now. Focus on a white door, where you're going to be able to see the Lord today. He is right in front of you. Hold on and wait. His doorway to heaven will appear. Ask and you shall receive. As bad acting as the interpreter has been through his life, he knows that if he can see so much inside of the holy spirit on a whim, you'll be able to see exactly the same vision of Christ.

Groups of pretty women parading around with flexible straw baskets of many ripe fruits have made their way to people, who've taken some as a gift. An actual banana was grabbed hold of by a shiny dark haired woman. One particular lady who carried the gift basket in the heavens has very dark skin, suggesting she may have been from the Carribean. She could still be from there, just because she lives in heaven doesn't mean her heritage has escaped her. Very green grapes, yellow apples and gold pears are inside her basket. This is the most current news about the lady, since she arrived sharing her gifts inside of the holy spirit, also for those of us interested in knowing. She walks forward and admires just two stalks of growing corn because that's all there is. One kernel of corn has a tinge of golden light shining upon it.

She removed one stalk of corn, while not noticing her shucking the full piece, because of her brilliant fast pace of doing things in heaven, she offers the vegetable on a glossy white plate. Her beautiful brown eyes made the interpreter forget about the corn for a minute. She is extremely happy. Another one of those beautiful people in heaven relaxing peacefully.

A black man comes in the spirit with very curly hair, kept up better than most. His dark beard and mustache are silky smooth. He comes wearing a white robe, and of all things a super long, and twice the normal width to the dark necktie to boot. But it's shiny. It's a big one. He isn't a clown. He has dark eyes with glimmering gold light touching the pupil's edge. But why does he take two gold eggs and suspend them in mid-air? To top that off another egg appears sunny side up. Why in the spirit, right? There is a white one, a brown one, and another white egg split in two, that having a layer of sunlight covering the first half. The saintly black man has a very tight left fist showing. On each side of his hand eggs suddenly appear, without opening them up. A white one on his right, and an actual whole golden egg is leaning against the other side of his closed hand. His long robe just turned all black, finely worn to suit his taste. Take a second to think about how he could do that inside of a split second. He bows down in prayer, but a humble man that he is, faithfully looking up to the Lord while praying.

His hands are pressed together now. For a black man, it's a mystery as to why his hands have changed to all white, more the color of some people's flesh. Perhaps God is in the light. Suddenly though, his hands are golden. And this spirit is interested in flowers like the rest of God's people in the light. He is entranced by the scent of a white carnation held up to his face.

The spiritual man was a real mover. He leaves to somewhere. There's a cute little Weiner dog who is wondering nearby. Him being the color of a hotdog is probably the reason why he was named as such. How strange, the dog taking the last visitor's place. A white light encircles the long dog. His head is quite visible, and he looks prepared to be transported somewhere into the light, while a furry black dog has come to his side to watch. He will be going on the whirling white light ride in heaven. The light becomes thick. His left ear hangs down over the edge of the cloud. His brown eyes and nose is what else we can see of him, right when the light leaves a strong indentation of his features, which was suggesting that he is ready to fly.

Bursts of strawberry red, cool blue and white rays of light bring some joy, mainly because of bright colors and influence God and Jesus have in the spirit world. Children's faces are camouflaged with these sudden colorful bursts, but you can still recognize their faces behind each arrangement. They remind you of Mardi Gras people at a younger age. The boy standing in a placid white light is blowing a small yellow bubble from his lips. That's some strange looking bubble gum. He pushes his chest out, stronger and stronger with all of his might.

The bubble is growing larger than your normal bubble that's for sure. He has both hands holding up the bubble in front of his face, but he still has it inside of his mouth. The kid is watching it enlarge up into the air, to where the bubble is bigger than himself now. Shortly the bubble will carry him away if he isn't careful. He turns his head and is trying to convey, by using his hands that he is tying a knot at the end of his balloon. It was that all along, and not bubble gum. One thing the boy has confirmed, there is definitely air inside of the holy realm, heaven. The boy who seems to be in his childhood has raised both knees since he has developed his own technique of flying by grabbing firmly beneath the bottom of his big yellow balloon. He has gone up into the light. New visitors have joined within the world of spirit communication, from their own promised land, to the earthly level, where their extended family becomes all knowing.

They are very much intended on saying what's on their mind, through spiritual and soulful dialect. They have mentioned a group of five helpers who have taken a seat at the inner whirling white light as members of a special delegated group. The white curling light flows right to their fingertips, but they're very much up and over the entire sculptured cloud which is much like a round conference table. They have a soothing gold eternal light glowing inside of the circle of friends who are spread apart around the perimeter, working at their seat. They have a need to find a way to send a message to the world. All five are studying matter inside of a glowing gold light which takes on the appearance of a microscope. Unbelievably, while trying to figure out what's happening, the Lord appeared inside of a pure pink vibration of light. He is harmonizing with the group of five. And the Holy Bible appears now. The spine was decorated with gold lettering. On black, gold is good. Then again, they're telling us to study the Bible. Their first message was delivered with help from the Lord. They would like to think that the spiritual message was carried. Palms matching up in the spirit with fingers twisting lightly means to cleanse your hands from any evildoing. That has to be what they convey, or else they would have kept their visual messaging to themselves if there wasn't a need for us to hear from them again. Research is needed seems to be the special message regarding the microscope.

The Lord wants us to sit comfortably with ease. From Him to you and me. Oh, you got to be kidding? Nope! The tiniest and cutest little baby angels you've ever set your big brown and blue peepers on, have just arrived to meet with your approval. You'll twist your neck and head around and above your shoulder blade a bit in disbelief, if you see them for the first time. There were three special angelical darlings flittering their delicate wings higher and higher to maintain altitude in heaven. They really do gleam in golden "light" color. That makes sense, they're inside of the holy spirit, and the golden ringlet of a halo, pings, in place above their adorable heads. Softer and a bit larger golden wings back up their first set which are still gleaming brightly. Those in back arrive without earlier notice, very enhanced. Smoother than smooth in much softer golden light. Black robes and tiny white buttons was the Lord's idea for the three. Their hair is shoulder length, considering how small they are, the trio is very unique with saffron light upon the strands of their hair. Each baby angel has a secret to reveal. While the word "secret" appears, they're about to give away each one that they're holding inside of their very gladdening hearts.

A pure white baby grand piano sits before the first little angel, who is someone's son. He likes to play the piano. His mouth is in the shape of a peanut with soft white light coming out from the inside of his soul. The second angel is a boy, and he is a real tiny little fellow, that he is. The angelic wings never have gotten in the way of him shooting hoops. That's unusual, yes, but he shows the hoop and basketball. Over on his side, you can do anything you think can be done. The third angel, she is a sweet little girl wearing very pink lipstick. Perhaps she wanted to be like her mother. She is happy too. She can make the boys fly along side of her when she wants. Flowing gold light over the white flowery pedestal came from the darling little angelic girl standing at the narrowing, splendorous base. How were we sure she was there? The pedestal was in heaven. The very tip of her sparkling golden wing pointing to the slender stand.

Three holy Bibles are being read by each small angelic child now. The Bibles with gold lettering were opened in between their wings and hands. This wonderful group of three are as captivating as any group or individual in the higher continuance of life. Angels delight you. Pink and white cotton balls pop up in the scenery. Hard telling if any pink cotton balls really existed in our lifetime, unless these were the only ones now known of. The angels can neatly tuck their Bibles under their wings when need be. With a golden ringlet halo, there is where one of the two angelical boys shows how he can do that. It is non-offensive to the Lord that these Holy Bibles be treated as such when carried about. The boy's golden halo goes completely out. No brighteners at all, except for a little bit of a dimmer white oval light inside of the outer black ring.

And he didn't just do that. Oh yes he did! The boy with Rosie red cheeks placed the Bible on top of his head. Suddenly gestures inside of the holy spirit suggested that he nearly doubled over so fast with laughter, that when it took place, the boy's comparably similar gold wings pointed downward. We are still wishing his halo would brighten again. Those darn little angels with their secrets. They still have the miraculous ability to grow in size. Them being way up in heaven.

The piano shown to play was very small, until the Lord just now changed all that. The width of the piano is huge. The angels haven't left us, they can be seen resting their faces beneath a white billowing light cloud. Inside of a cloud, the Lord's brilliantly shining pointy gold crown won't stop glowing. The other white cloud, where the angelic babies are, golden wings are propping it up beneath its whirling wonder. A whole soft white candle inside of the cloud is showy. And now over to the right of the whirling masses, new white angels are being peacemakers on the inside of clouded light. There's golden light coming from our Lord's crown. It covers everyone and radiates so much pureness and light over them. They became thrilled by the sight. The little boy's halo has finally brightened with a dash of gold light, so much that the top looked like a rounded neon sign. Quite nice for an angel to be wearing a powerful halo.

Just another huge caramel white, fluffed up angel wing created out of the heavens to sit and look pretty. Yes it is just that. The Lord reminded the interpreter to be truthful about what was seen. His magical performances are deeply admired before commenting. When you get to the other side, you're not always going to need a specific guide there, unless one is appointed. Now another angel's wing is most becoming. Although the outer lining is black, the creation appeared to be a drawing pressed deeply into a spiritual canvas. Insightfulness is what we will benefit from of the soft white light, and brilliance behind the singular wing, which does in fact have a softer orange disc of smoother light on the inside. If the first wing suits your fancy more, then you're very much into the mere beauty of heaven's creations. Just an educated guess. However, the second wing has more to look at and probe. It suggests there is a light from beyond where angels have a strong quality, whether formed of dynamic light, fuller like the other angels, or not, each sign from God is spellbinding. The caramel white sheds a beautiful path of light to where you would feel at ease walking directly into that light. The angelical creation above is now shedding the pleasant orange rays of light from the center of a wing, cleansed in the holiest light which had led up to the creation. While believing more in the message with typical deep spiritual meditation into the world of spirituality, the greater golden ornate structure to the Lord's armrest on His throne becomes intuited. The image of the brain appears, and the word "complex" shows.

Yes, the whirling white light ride in heaven would be common. Not thought to be though. God is ever so remindful. Now His gold crown sits on top of the whirling white light. Just when we thought something may be pointing to unfairness by misleading, that would be totally absurd. All of the gold to the Lord's crown covered the whirl light below. Solid gold and Godly. The whirling light went from white to gold, and our wonderful Lord's crown is frosty. That didn't last long, the crown is all gold again. You should see it. Worth a mint in gold. The Lord wants us to ask Him to bring us to heaven. That brought some joy knowing we can trust Him as a "buddy." Not a poor choice of words, taking in consideration, some answers come through prayers, out of body experiences, dream states and these non-stop visions.

One well cushioned white resting place similar to a car seat was just revealed in the massive whirling light. But the milder white light inside will open your mind up so greatly, you'll think a new drug had been invented to calm your nerves. Two tunnels of golden light, the first at one o'clock, and the other at seven, that is an example in our well-timed world, to help understand their position in the spirit of eternity, whereas they're sending penetrating gold light, covering the ride. Not a radioactive sight, but you'd think as such only in a glorious way.

The hand of God or the Lord is upon the seat, overlapping it. In plain view our Master's hands cup beneath the entire seat now. What do you make of that happening thus far? The Lord knows it is somewhat hard to comprehend, from your view, but it will be delightful travel into the spirit if you ask Him. You are granted admission into heaven. The best way to explain what the spirit just did was if you could visualize a gigantic stretch of golden surface on your visit to a colorful wonderland, curving on the way through, your whirling white light ride, decorated in golden sunlight will be stupendous to feel inside. Since we are raised inside of the light, we'll always feel great enjoyment. Someone is going to make our day right now.

Bushy white eyebrows and closed lids appear. The center of a forehead, nose, and mouth are completely white too. Mint green eternal light glows on both sides of this remarkable spirit. Eyes have opened, and they are as brown and wet as chocolate. Parted hair down the middle has been brushed back, or at least tamed very well to stay in place, nearly shoulder length. His full mustache covering his top lip arches slightly over and upon his manly beard. The light is the way. He is a follower of Christ who carries such a small, but very meaningful candlestick in his hand, which sent out a sparkling glow around its flame. A larger version of that candle stands on each side of the spirit guest. He has cloudy white shoes, similar to moccasins, not on his feet, but tilted downward inside his hands as to be offering the gift. We can wear soft shoes in heaven, especially a shoe which looks like a tan moccasin. Naturally from the light riches, claimed much later in life after life. The gifts will be numerous as you sit before the Lord and God, you'll wonder how they've created everything for you and your family so quickly.

In heaven there are the glorious pathways lined with picket fences, made from sparkling silver and gold, profoundly enriched with sparkling colors of eternal light. A man with curling brown hair, which tends to straighten a bit from thinner layers rubbing up against them, has been enjoying the trip in heaven laying on his back. He's inside a whirling white light, face up to the heavens, as he is smiling passing others. He is up in the air just a little behind the long sparkling fence. He points upward with his left hand. Four white spiraling lights which seem harmless have occupants resting peacefully, one young man leaning out, while laying on his side. Likely to get a good view of the man we saw first. The four people passing by were much smaller in extent to where spiritual magnitude is often exercised openly.

Discipline is a must inside of the holy spirit. God is very much concerned how organized everyone is, that's why some become very overwhelmed by His sudden movements when He walks, especially when He and the Lord want obedience. We will be on our knees thanking Jesus that He is our Lord, all of His doing. The blissfulness prevails.

Such a rapturous white light beneath our feet. If not white it shall be golden. Perhaps the colors of the rainbow, whirling beneath the tremendous white light which carries you home. In the spirit, God is demonstrating. With added colors too. The whirling white light is turning gold, and blue in another section, then green and orange. The blue has whirling white light. There are white polka dots inside of the gold glowing mass, and a gold castle awaits your presence which is all visible. Pink vibrant light spreads over the white light. It has many gold pointed stars. Each color and design lifts higher, after yet another huge whirl wind of light takes on that full image of gold with white polka dots and so on. A long and very smooth pink stem of light shoots out from the bottom of the ride. Once straight and solid, the pink expands giving creative beauty one more chance to be glorified.

Billowing orange clouds of smoke simulated by light pour out from a gigantic train's engine. It has pulled into heaven with a happy fellow leaning from a cutout window. Seems like there are a few of these trains flowing through the railways up there. The train's engine has gone miniature on us, because when the interpreter looked up and saw the Lord's chest, and white robe covering His knees on the throne, down below where the King's feet rest the train is still present.

A normal size yellow butterfly grows bigger, and then much larger. But the entire butterfly was changing quicker even more so. Its wingspan is recognizable even though the butterfly has become somewhat thin from losing its color. An outline of every feature still remains in full view. The eyes are huge, no kidding. Why they have the color of yellow in an outer ring surrounding the dark pupil is quite fascinating. A wonder with them as they change things around. Gospel music is very entertaining in the spirit.

The Lord is allowing this to be said about Himself. He is directing hundreds and thousands of people, if not more, as the choir director. Funny, He glanced over His left shoulder like He knew us well already. The tan color baton gently waving in the spirit to the finer points of music rendered helps the Lord listen very close to each and every sound in symphony, as directed. He just lined his baton up full center upon His face. His blue eyes were focused in to this side where we live, but we should count on Jesus setting His heart on helping His music choir more. Even though His choir can't wait, the Lord gives us His complete attention. More to come.

Little white paws visible in the light, and on this side of life at the same time. Blue light glows. A bunny sitting in the white spotlight more over and into his spiritual land of fun and excitement again. God only knows the heavens is where our life really begins, that being of total awareness of who we are and how we have come to know our Lord and His Father in their sanctuary. The mighty golden lion the Lord just revealed in the light was grand, not frightening. What if God could make Himself into a lion? After visiting with the king of beasts, it's no wonder God created such an animal. Inside of the light the furry animal sat upright, gleaming in gold and simply resting in peace. But was God just visiting us as a lion? And a second lion appears in mid-air with a lion's roar, his sharp teeth were showing. Of the same breed, but the first lion has a thick illustrious golden halo over his head, stretching from one ear over to the other. The lion coming in the light is viewing a huge swath of peaceful white light from heaven, where his curiosity has risen, a new place to roam freely, next life, where perhaps he'll have the same glorious aura of light covering him, fully.

Five white inner tubes of light are issued in heaven, but why do you think they are doing that there? A woman with super lengthy dark hair to her shoulders, luckily, she has beautiful golden light shining through it as she rests inside of one of the buoyant tubes of circular light. She looks to the heavens where golden light streams brightly down upon her, and when it has drawn our attention to her very soul, sparkles of gold has covered her head in the shape of a see-through, rounded lamp shade. She is rising in position heading forward with the white inner light growing wider and wider. The white light is very peaceful, but she desires to lift herself out from the spiritual ride. She presses down on the circular edge of whiteness from the amazing ride, which picked her up, and now she seems to be able to freely release herself. Finally giving thought back to the other white inner tubes of light. There are people inside of them, using them in water. They have informed that they're using them while swimming. Rest assure it was for a reason though.

At a new doorway beginning to shed an awful lot of pink light mostly outside, back on the inside a soft baby blue color spreads out, near and far. There are many doors in heaven. The Lord is doing that thing He does with His index finger, pointing to His chin while seated. Softest golden light known in eternity covers Him, but not shedding. Wish you were there to see Him?

A young boy holding a radio to his ear is whistling, a telling sign from puckering his lips. Why music from a radio, and why doesn't he just pick out a tune from the heavenly realm of endless possibilities? He wants us to know that he has knowledge of how sound works when it comes to music. He placed his index finger beneath his chin, like the Lord, and shortly thereafter, golden music notes flowed in rhythm to what he was thinking about inside of his mind. He's in yellowy gold light with radio in his left hand still, and the other hand is very effective for him to be snapping and swishing his fingers around to the tempo. The boy loves music. When asked, "What does he listen to?" "Our music," was the holy spirit's response using visible words. The strange thing was the radio had a long antenna. The boy knows how to do special tricks too.

After passing the radio on over to his right hand, he suddenly twists his wrist and tosses the small box into the air. And the radio stopped in mid-air, where plenty of soft gold light fills the heavens, and the light of God turned to sunshine. Seeing that varnishing act was interesting. Nice to know the boy's bowing down inside of the holy spirit. He is pleased, that's why. No serious bellyache for that little boy. He bowed with his arm over his stomach is why you heard that, aforementioned communiqué. He is needed elsewhere. He has something large in his hand that he carries by its black handle. You're not going to believe it, but he is carrying a transportable radio, much bigger than what he came here with. Spirit people have visited with all sorts of crazy things in their hands, funny to mention that, but it's true.

You know you're on the right track when you tell the Lord how beautiful His angelic children are. A baby with such a large and spectacular crystal halo. With a guardian close by, whoever is in charge, that person sways the child up as if to be handing the little angel to someone, or to be teaching the little one how to fly with her extra rounded off honey golden wings. They kind of remind you of gold snowshoes. Maybe a first in the spirit to be seen from their side of life. Fine and dandy when you see the signs and wonders, but doesn't it make you feel a little bit on edge when an image appears and you can't quite put your finger on it? A woman with gorgeous shoulder length blonde curls of hair looks up to the next small angel baby learning how to get on in life inside of the spirit land. And she has the same color of golden wings, but they are arching back instead of outward. The baby girl has blonde curls of hair too.

Her eyes are brown and pure. The woman watching the child may be her mother. They are close to one another, and with matching hair, there's no doubt that they're related someway. Baby's wings are working all on her own now. The expression in her eyes is of amazement. Floating up above on her very own is priceless. Her cute puckered lips suggest she is very much surprised indeed. Heaven is more peaceful than we have ever thought it to be. And the serene feeling we'll acquire with the Masters of light will be much more than just a passing notion.

Mint green and a baby blue soft light. They go together well when coming from the Lord, like He just had shown. With the Lord looking downward, likely here to earth, as seen now, He comes back inside of the softly whitened, and gold light. And He was asked in prayer a question. After believing that He was carrying a child on His back with small golden wings, an answer came from Him. "They are my wings," was shown with spiritual wording from the Lord inside a lucid vision while visiting with Him. He believes we are enlightened by the light when spoken about. A pink vibration glowed, but after it went away it returned, this time much brighter. Let's take a breather for a moment. Try squeezing your eyes together tightly to see what comes to you inside of the light from Jesus. Make them close tight now. Only for a few seconds though, unless you'd care to meditate deeply in the spirit. You should have seen many colorful spirit vibrations of eternal light appear. Try again if you don't first succeed.

Cute and simply the best. Here we have for your enjoyment a small angel with dark curls of hair. He is laying on his tummy enjoying peace while upon his floating white cloud, which gracefully tends to glide and whirl upward. He looks up to see what's going on, between heaven and the physical world. He needs to put a shirt on. All kidding aside, if the Lord wishes for him to be a babe of comfort and joy that's their business. Thankfully that's all they reveal, meaning from his tummy on up. But he is a little angel like the rest of the children. His halo glows like the top of a lightbulb. He turned over quickly to see what was coming down from the heavens. A red poppy flower and tiny sparkles of gold dust from the heavens are upon him.

Within his comfort zone two solid white harps sit almost back to back, with the high arches looking like a guardian angel in a way. Soft white light glows inside of the harps, and as usual, beautiful gold strings. A tremendous amount of projecting white light upon gold flowers and leaves keeps on coming. One flower alone has been left all gold. What were suppose to have been the tops of the leaves popping out from the white blanket of light, turned into angel wings. The golden flower with leaves above the angelic presence has a white cross in the middle for a relaxing design. And the round pan of gold with a nugget inside, and an almost identical item without the treasure is a comparison being made. Your treasure is in the Lord's heart. He is relating that to you, through the interpreter. His people will know how to think and feel without the interpreter, but the Lord uses all of us in a special way.

Don't cry Jesus. He has His hands cupped with His face in them. On His throne, Jesus sits there bent over weeping. And why is that so? He will be asked in prayer. He says, "If I lose you I would be unhappy." Again, visible wording showed. We need to love Him, because the Lord especially loves everyone. His hands are folded. The gold radiating light spears coming out from on top of His interlaced hands are amazing to see. The Lord does help you open your mind more. Think of it as mostly clear.

Kids are going nuts in the light over a ride just now coming into view. That will lift their spirit dramatically. The ride is very white. There is a woman relating she can cry in heaven, but those feelings are overridden with joy. Really funny stuff seen. The kid's rides are of dogs and cats heads, all white for now, and we would think they were created from clouds. Kids sit inside behind the face of the animal. Little white blocks of light appear, so it's more than likely probable that they can pedal them manually. The small ones sit upon the whirls of white light, too. They are so high up in heaven. What a glimpse. A girl with straw blonde hair with straight bangs is trying to listen up close to the big fluffy white dog with dark eyes.

Confirmed with the Lord as correct. She is riding into the beautiful wedges of golden light, but not without leaving us something to think about. She is holding a golden horseshoe in her left hand. She must be wishing us, "good luck." The bottom fringe of her angelic white gown is highlighted with many arrangements of glittering gold. She is either putting something good to eat inside her mouth, otherwise she is giggling away by gesturing.

A few frosty and glowing half-moons have appeared. Now faces of spiritual saintly people have arrived in the light, and those half-moons are very much a part of their appearance. They are halos. The long bearded saints are deep thinkers, debaters if you will. Two stand across from one another, both holding out scrolls, although one is smaller in width. But what they're doing is planning your destiny. That's what they show, but you can't be one hundred percent sure, because you can't see them and be able to tell if, that's the whole truth behind them visiting. A very tall white candle and wick appear before the white robed gents. Then the whirling tunnel of white light which looks like a blast to walk in through. There are three ivory staircases where each saint has chosen to walk up to. Their backs are turned as they have become more of a distant image with themselves preparing to walk upon the stairs. They have become much more larger in appearance though, a sudden change, whereas their shoulders are very masculine, and what's strange is the three are almost side by side now. What a powerful presence!

The mysteries of heaven unravel. With backs still turned it is more obvious than not that the two holy people on the right have taken a position of kneeling, while the saint on the left has remained standing. A gold crown begins to glow up over them, as if they were actually visiting a special altar meant for the Lord. A soothing pink and orange light gives off those good feelings inside. And that came in front of them at the shrine. Wonderful designing inside of the kingdom of red against black swirling colors add to the majestic decor. Feel rest assured that God's and the Lord's handwork is so artistic that mere words doesn't do it justice at all. Masterful once again. More of a finding in the spirit for us.

A couple of brilliant angels entered within solid manifestation of oval faces, black in color, and white chests that of dress wear. They wear robes. White halos for them, and if we don't get the glowing light coming from the edges of their eyes, they surely do. It's peaceful and white, while their eyes are really very crystal clear and brown. They feel we must think that they are real. Both of the guys are pushing down on solid yellow light, and added to the shape is that of logs, used basically as an example. Instantly swirls of brown color enhances the objects like slithering chocolate. And they feel we'd like to know more. The angelical male on the right has touched the top of the unusual pole of sorts, and as he does some golden light shines upon it, changing the object white, with silver glitter forming in a straight line, from the very top on down to the bottom. He tilts the creation to one side, careful not to let it fall over. Down near the bottom there are very jagged edges on the side. And out of the heavens a piece of white cake appears on a plate that his friend took. He had turned the solid light that had been pressed down upon into a tall frosting cake with drizzling silver slivers of light. His angelic friend even played out the scene, where he had secretly bent down to remove a piece. Better they do that in heaven than get in trouble. As for the other beam of solid yellow light with brown swirls, it remained the same. One huge cake which is probably ready for his friend to take a bite out of.

As the interpreter sits and ponders. Thought was given to the people in heaven who wear the wreaths upon their heads with the bright green leaves and colorful flowers. While seeking the kingdom a woman with brown hair is looking down from the heavens, wearing a wreath with mostly white flowers and vibrant green leaves. At least the Lord can read minds and every thought, and to pinpoint with great accuracy when to reveal. He wants this done right for everyone interested in His plan. That was service with a smile and none too soon. A little girl holding a white bouquet of flowers stands about four feet tall. Too young to be the heaven child that she is. Or is she? Her wreath is special, and even though there are only two white flowers, they have dashes of redness on the edges of very few of the petals.

It's spiritual guidance, and that's how it is done. A group of four young children, close to the flower girl's age and height stand in a semicircle, and they face forward for all to see. They have flower wreaths in their hair, too, some flowers red and white, even very close to each other. They have been intermeshed. The connection in our brain to God's, again, that proves we are one.

A true but unbelievable sight for the unfortunate few who disbelieve in the Lord's immediate presence in your life. The Lord has such a beautiful glowing powder blue, glorified halo, outside the white one which is closer to His hair. He says, using visible words, "Tell them what you know." From below the Lord all around, and quite far above Jesus, every other small candle is the same blueness with a white flickering wick of light. However, those in between are white stick candles with a powder blue flame of light. If we studied this carefully, those candles were in the larger shape of either an angel wing, or that of a beautiful harp curving upwardly and beyond.

Behind the Lord, in a distance the shining gold castle belonging to Jesus and His family. It has a golden ball of light which is glowing at one of the doors, it's believed. In any event, the beaming light is present. They're telling us when we have passed on into the light we shall enter into the kingdom, where there are trillions of people who really populate the majestic spirit land. Not only the kingdom of God awaits our arrival, loved ones in heaven have estimated when that will be. Right now this very minute, people up above have such great expectation of their cherished family member's arrival, they're toes tense a little bit, to where many stand together about to fall forward from the excitement of being joined eternally. Three family members in a semi-circle can be seen from here, so the interpreter knows first hand how overjoyed people will be when that happens. Let's hope it isn't too soon. They think it is in no time at all though.

While watching an unexpected male Indian examine his lengthy braided hair, laying gently over his left shoulder, you have to wonder what's so magical about him. Seeing him is plenty considering he is a visible spirit, and someone who can become invisible at a glance. But he's here inside of the holy spirit. He holds his hand against the side of his head, because he is very proud of his hairstyle. He's really excited. The Indian guide twirls his hand around in a small circle, creating a whirling white cloud from light. First one hand is covered, then both become filled with white clouds which eventually travel down the full length of his arms, before covering almost the rest of his eternal soul. The orange glowing light on his left cheek is soft, though, and most surprisingly, he's an energetic Indian with a fondness for real people. Part of his arm pushes out from the light as he seems to whirl in an ease of motion, as much to notice, one, two, three, and even a forth movement. On account of him stepping up a little faster. But the light is so smooth. You know what God is doing? Every time our Indian friend's arm pokes out of the heavier whirling light ride a golden cross sparkles. Our heavenly Father is so serious about showing us the cross representing life, which our Lord has awarded us with, that He lets it shine on all occasions as well.

A large brown cello with a woman facing it directly has a close listener with her leaning into the instrument. With white light filling out her long hair and a quick wink she gave from her brown eyes, consciously, she let her gender be known. Listen to the music. Enjoy the sound it gives you. She smells a full leaf yellow flower and lets it go, flowing in the spirit it lands before the interpreter inside of his livingroom. Of a vision. One foot then two feet appear side by side. Sandals were seen too. Was that the woman inside of the holy spirit coming closer, or was that Lord? Now how could the Lord be standing near us? Easy! The woman is visibly standing nearby, not as much of a spiritual vision, anymore, she's an incredible spirit. Heaven doesn't have a traveling agency, travelers in the light are "helpers" for encouraging people to believe in spirit communication and prophecy.

You know that you're chosen as the special people of the Lord when you have heard of the whirling white light ride in heaven. Others who've yet learned of these wondrous, joy-filled rides are very special too. A lady with dark curls of hair kneels before the Lord. She is covered in the whirls of white light, although her hands, and from the neck on down, the sloping angelic robe she has on is that much smoother in appearance. As for her covered hands, she appears to be wearing a white "muff." Hardly for warmth, but likely there is much comfort for her still. Her knees fit on a square white light, similar to a kneeling pad. Now the worshiper holds her left hand to her ear while turning her head, and immediately a swath of new white light appears near her face. Then with her other hand and ear she repeats the very first action, and subsequently another swath of brightened white light appeared near her hand and face. She wants us to listen.

An open book with white pages with small black print reveals a thick Bible. How that was told was by her and the Lord bringing the Bible in the light for a view, when after closing the good book, the name was seen of the front cover, much like how the Lord has represented His word before, a demonstration in heaven which can be seen here on earth, through amazing visuals.

The Lord is precise with His actions in the spirit. The children of heaven find it amusing ringing smaller and even the much larger gold and silver bells before them. Dressed in white robes adorning black choir bows fit for the occasion, boys and girls test out the sounds to each bell. They bells sit upon a long white slab of soft light. A nice table. The children are very good natured. They want you to know they can make musical sound echo across heaven. Also, very few bells have been mentioned compared to how many in assortment they possess, and we'd be surprised by how they chime out loud. One of God's children, the same lady who was on the kneeling pad, had dipped her hands in through the bottom of her cotton candy like whirling white light mass, and in a snap, she created a solid heart for show. She desires to keep it at home, so deeply admired by her, anyone can see she is very proud of her artistry in heaven.

After making the perfect heart a very thin vaporous white light appears in front of her mouth. She brings that to life while also pointing to more whirling white light. From the bottom of the light, swirling design has created several small hearts, one by one, they developed into a solid heart, but every other one you could see through. They are all connected together by light. She busily goes to work adjusting it to each side of the large white heart that she has close by.

Naturally it fits on the top too. Nice golden light comes down from heaven and glows inside of the see-through hearts. That caused immediate surprise for her, only because the light was a little unexpected in that manner. It's still hard to believe she is holding up the artwork, that alone is "not" from this world. The golden rays now shoot up and out over the bridge of hearts, and beneath the solid white heart. Which leads us back to her returning to the Lord to offer Him this gift by His feet. He gladly accepted her love offering and rests it upon His lap. If you can believe such a story you'll feel comforted to know, the Lord just covered His daughter with a blanket of His white light which is filled with an immense feeling of love. We will feel more free inside.

The other side of life is suggesting that we release ourselves from our troubles. Pressed together hands do appear inside of the holy spirit, not uncommon to see, and so when we pray to the Lord a change is what to expect. You reject the thought of being helped inside by the holy spirit, and they understand. People in the light are saying we won't be the same when we arrive, and that we'll be relieved from our duties at last. Expect to be put on center stage for all to admire. The Lord has many unexpected ways for you to be met by your loved ones. A tap on the shoulder or the precious soul so dear to you inside of your family, one of the cherished members may even walk up to you with a beautiful fresh bouquet of flowers. He demonstrates in the spirit many things and good ideas for you to be learning from right now. These out of body experiences come with the presence of our Lord guiding the interpreter carefully.

A special garden of dark red and purple flowers hang in an open arch on the special pathway inside of heaven. A curly haired blonde with soft golden light touching her hair is wearing a small white bow attached on the side of her head, and she points to inside of the garden, wanting us to join her there. The Lord would really be the only one to truly know how He planned this unexpected meeting, between her and the woman's mother. She is cheek to cheek with her mother who seems more of a white light spirit figure of a lady, who hasn't seen her in a very long time. So when she pointed inside of the garden, she was with the Lord too. He was covered in white light, and with a golden light going off and then back on, slowly, heightening his facial hair, the emphasis on Him and the blonde with her mother in the garden was a delight. Mostly, she was overwhelmed is why she looked back to the Lord and had pointed to mother.

Everlasting white light fills the heavens once more bringing peace and love. The blue streaks of light passing by seem to evaporate into thin air, but the Lord would never destroy His own light, therefore He uses it wisely elsewhere. Good thinking is helpful when working with the Lord inside of the holiest spirit known to all. The holy spirit holds our utmost attention as He creates four solid white circle of white light, one above, the next below it more, and the remaining circles on the left and right. That's where not only does He suspend each ball of light, but He managed to send forth radiating light spears from each one. It doesn't end, a new glowing white ball of light in the center suddenly appears while Jesus goes to work on thrilling us. Inside of the middle a burst of golden light is interesting. And clearly for all to see, the Lord's thorn wreath is tilted on an angle, resting upon a stick cross. Jesus made a yellow flower bloom from the outer left corner of His sacred wreath crown. Just absolute peacefulness to feel in His very holy presence. Praise the Lord.

A brown haired boy who looks familiar from one other visitation comes back. He has a lot of hair, somewhat overlapping his ears. He looks very friendly while wearing a white choir robe with a black bow. And a furry dark dog with white paws is along side of the boy. What does the dog do? He is standing on his hind legs, but not as a beggar. A white smidgen of light appeared on the lad's index finger, and as he stands on a side view, he wiggled his index finger around and vanilla ice-cream fills a cone up. Someone obliged the boy for wanting a chocolate topping and went so far as to cover all of the delicious treat. Right out of the heavens, brown chocolate. Even if you dislike the following it is funny to listen to. The boy has a whirling white car ride he sits at now. His dog, paws up on the steering wheel inside of his little car. A smaller model and quite sporty in a way. Now that happening up in heaven is hilarious.

They went somewhere heaven like, and the boy assists his pet from the smaller cloud car, lifting him beneath his front legs. A very fluffy white angel wing is a symbol sitting by the small wall in front of a secret entrance to a place that has to be special. The wall was white shaped like a cloud. The dog and child have had white cloud rings around them ever since they have arrived.

A nice pat on the dog's back as he looks up to the boy for guidance. Awe-inspiring blue eternal light is so far in the distance from where they stand, yet, overhead it was only a mere stone's throw away. A sparkling gold angel sits nearby. Wow, that's all. The boy snatches a pure white airplane from the sky and giggles with irresistible laughter. He points to a rocket and the word, "mishap" appears. Having to do with the past, even the little boy has knowledge of tragic events from our side. One thing for sure he holds his hands in a "v-shape" on each side of his face. He knows what it is like to lose loved ones. Small gold and white sparkly crosses decorate the scenery in abundance with some of the crosses inside of white circles.

If we were blind or deaf, we could still understand and feel the spirit of God when He approaches. The movements made by Him are very keenly done, besides swiftly. There is such great royalty in our own names. That comes from Jesus and His Father. Then comes Mary. So you think She'll pop up inside of Her holy spirit right at this moment? You're right, you have the spiritual knowledge of such a beautiful holy Mother inside of your heart, so deeply enriched that your own personal feelings for Mary have been growing inside of your heart and mind for many days now. This is what She wants you to believe in Her for, loving everyone inside of the spiritual realm, and all people in our land who respect her willingly. She resides in splendid grandeur of Her Son, and Father too.

The interpreter nods to the Virgin Mary, and was merely stunned at the same time. Never has She appeared like this, firstly. Her glittering silver crown, very large indeed, sits inside of Her hands tilted forward in a mild orange light. What is so remarkable and breathtaking about Mary is that She is so free of a loving and Godly spirit, that She comes on a whim with Her long dark hair, curling, slightly passing Her shoulders. How can this royal lady do that? She did right here and right now. She has plenty to offer us. Anyone on God's green earth would have loved to see what Mary just did. She made Her Son's gold cross appear on Her face. Right in the middle and across Her pink cheeks, She did. The golden glow and the cross has 'such wonderful and great meaning that She is cupping Her hands, bringing them close to Her heart. She is now wearing a very nice grey robe with puffy white flowers imprinted upon it, unless they are real. She is wearing Her diamond studded crown now, but what is more striking is the softness inside of Her blue eyes. A look of endless beauty. The loveliness of them is unreal.

When you see a crown inside of the light, we'd probably expect to see a beard and mustache too. Mary's face is smooth, much to do with ageless beauty. She says, "Im caring for my children." Words are visible inside of the holy spirit, a mentioning that has been acknowledged well in the past. A small red heart, a string of sparkling gold hearts and a solid white one appears around Her throne. She is bottle feeding babies milk once again. They know who She is as they feel the love of a Mother. Mary smiles and She really is enjoying this. Many dark blue patches of light appear deep in the background, behind Her and the children.

She says, "Tell them I am here." Mary holds a yellow flower in Her hand, but in a split second, one of the babies grabs hold of it. Mary is giving. But Mary has Her way and holds it with the child, bringing the scented flower close to the child's face. This is very nice of Mary. She shares the yellow flower with the other infant, one who is so small that the babe in arms needs the same kind attention as what the other child received. Being told to wait on sharing more from the Virgin Mary was a little bit of a surprise. She and the Lord have brought us in even closer.

The Lord will lead us further into the light. Several oval whirling white light rides are available once again. They look like hanging tire tree swings, without the tires, instead what we can see are children sitting inside of the rides, where they can hold on from the inside of the cloudy seat. Children are hanging out from inside as the whirling light rolls up on over their heads, and back again, beneath them, so much that it is a gigantic seat for them to rest upon. However, there is a soft beam of solid white light extending from the top of each child's ride to the high heavens. One ride has two golden lights on the front. Another has a blue light similar to a bright bulb. Others vary in color from orange to pink.

One of the little boys slipped out from the whirling white light ride and is now on a small yellow pony, holding onto the red handles. They are pegs. You'd think that the blonde girl was from Holland, she wears a shapely black hat with a silver star on front. Her white light ride was raised, but after a sudden turn it went horizontal. The light thickens, whirling. Soon the whirls change pattern and returns to the original form, whirling up and down, back around again, beneath her and back around in front of the adorable girl again. The spirit of the girl with stringy blonde bangs, highlighted by a small golden light, aglow upon her face, has gotten down off her ride and is levitating about, smoothly, and she is somewhere here in the heavens, where you wished that you could be on your worse or best day of your life. The feeling received from watching the Lord's children rests your mind at ease. That white light is ceremonious, and so peaceful. The young girl's robe is white light, remarkably true.

Whirling white light comes, one, two, three at a time, it arrived for many small children, a great wonder that can be seen, created from being wrapped around the Lord's great hands, floating downward in great amounts that have easily arrived for the children. That's one way they have received the rides. There's more knowledge to it than that.

Two very wide golden steps lead to a flat surface above which matches in color and grandness. Pink light is coming down from heaven like a soft spotlight shining upon the golden landing. A nice glowing sensation is part of the teaching. Two very mild golden teardrops are falling and when they land, bursts of soft light result in a couple of yellow baby chicks standing center stage now. An unusual way to be hatched, don't you think? Perhaps that is the way they travel around inside of the light. Maybe just this one instance. God was asked about if there were people who He thought shouldn't have been born. In separate patterns of soft white light, His message came through. "All were needed." Just those words appeared in black lettering. Enough to be clearly understood without having to ask Him why. You know what's really funny about heaven?

You could think about moving about from place to place with a jet pack strapped to your back. Not really something that will occur daily, but if that's what you'd wish for in the spirit, they'll arrange it for you. Something you need to know. You'll find yourself with others inside of the peaceful heavenly realm having a lot of fun, and you will be advised that the Lord would like to share an excited way of meditating, just right out of the blue. He will have you raised up inside of the holy spirit, by yourself, or even your family and friends will join in. Your soul will levitate from the soft surface of heaven and you'll find yourself with folded arms and legs in mid-air. In heaven you won't need any apparatus to hold you up in place. The peace of mind is so enormous. Let it never end. You won't feel alone. Even if it was just you sitting like a noble guru in the higher spiritual realm of greatness, your mind perceives all which is good.

No need to worry about having company because Jesus is there too. We will always be able to see Him, but if He chooses to let you meditate on happiness, and having a peace of mind, you shall know all which is holy from the other side of life. Love will fill your soul a thousand times more than which has already been granted unto you. We'll be at peace often because of the Lord.

The beauty in the spirit will astound you. As we meditate sitting up straight with our eyes opened or even shut, which is often the case, we can visit many places through the out of body traveling experience. We shall not remain in one place while we meditate, there are people and places to see using the strength of our Godly mind. So great that we are, we'll be able to even see what we are doing from a short or even a longer distance away. It sounds unusual going off into different directions, and still being able to watch our inner soul resting in the vibrant heavenly lights, through a higher meditative state that will be so very gentle.

Try to relax while you think. Soft white and golden eternal lights are spotty, and they continuously flash so quickly that they are non-bothersome. Wide golden adjoined archways appear this way, closer to the shape of tall church windows. Only white flowers hang loosely from outside of these arches. Lines of people form at each entrance. Mostly inside is where they belong congregating. Filled in the holy spirit a peaceful white light has fallen upon them. They await their turn to visit closely with the Lord. Why is that so when He is everywhere? There are many ways to see His children. One thing definite, the people covered in white light have all decided to pray to Him and likely to Father God while they visit in line. The people do turn from side to side, and they're very excited to meet their heavenly Father. Now the Lord shows the bottom structure to three white thrones, somewhat spread apart. Just because they are softly glowing in whiteness doesn't mean that the thrones are not golden.

A change made would be in their honor when it happens inside of the throne room. Up in the background, but behind each throne a blue dash of light rests above them. From left to right, inside of the first beautiful creation a silver cross appears. Inside of the middle creation a sparkling gold cross has been revealed and fully respected as well. Finally the third blue creation of light has a white cross centered inside of the eternal light. We must believe that Mary sits upon Her throne in ruling class too. Not the first thing that jumps out in the spirit, but the second were the two red hearts. They were small but very nice. The first vision was another pretty white flower, but the gold light, it was almost too intense to look at for more than a couple seconds. It couldn't have been because of them, though. Now a five foot golden cross comes in front of the center throne, but more came. The left white sleeve from a holy robe, that was direct. And that huge gold crown. Wow, is that ever big and exciting too. Jesus has a big face. A small pink heart was placed upon the Lord's left cheek, close to the top edge of His mustache, otherwise He put it there. His face is so pure you want to touch Him. Instantly the scenery changes and where Mother Mary, and where God and the Lord were sitting upon their thrones, inside through the golden archways of swirling vines and flowers a gold curtain, quite wide, seemed to close in front of them. They have opened way back in the heavens, which is a surprise, but after they have, the curtains have divided and were separated in back of all three thrones. Half of the curtain off to the far left, and the rest of it was hanging up far away over to the right. The thrones were smaller, but not even the interpreter should be the judge of that.

Three trails of baby blue light are leading up into higher areas of heaven. It is good to think of them as trails of light. The spirit world believes that is so. A black woman and two young people, who seem to be boys, have communicated they're wearing frosted white halos. They do look quite nice. One boy is smaller in height than the other. What do they want? All races reside in heaven. The spiritual woman, sure is the day is long, handed over a very shiny french horn for the tallest to play. He's wearing a black silk robe and a white carnation.

His siblings dress alike. Golden music notes flourish around the boy as he gives his all and all in blowing the horn. His cheeks are full of air to make sound come out. The mother stands proudly between both of her boys with an arm around each of them very affectionately. But why does she and the smaller boy have the golden u-shape harps attached to the front of themselves as carry-ons?

While she examines her harp, close at the bottom it gleams more than before, and now it's understood that it is light as a feather. An image of the Lord has come. He watches over the three people. Why would you think His face turned completely black, casting darkness upon His shoulder length hair, mustache, and especially over His beard? Even though the Lord appears this way, His color has brought the best out in people. That is because the Lord is in the image of His Father, therefore, God makes appearances inside of the Lord's holy spirit in a mysterious way. Folded prayer hands were just seen, and many words come too. "Pray for your friend's health," were visible words in the spiritual world. A man about the age of thirty sits cross-legged inside of the mild golden light meditating using prayer.

He has straight hair bangs. The saturation of light upon him makes it hard to determine his hair color, however, he does have a new way of prayer that we may take into consideration. Fold your hands into a ball, or with interlaced fingers. He left a space between his first index finger and two thumbs resembling a hole in his hands. As he prays, both folded hands raise up to his face, right to his ear now. The small hole between his fingers and thumbs pressed up to his ear as to be listening for a response from the Lord. Something we can do in prayer, and hopefully we'll hear our answer that we are waiting for. He returned his hands back to the front of his chest. A mild white light soothes his mind and soul, apart from remaining within a warmth of golden light.

Remain still in peace is advised. There is a way to use more of our brain, unlocking it to enjoy many more mysteries in life, especially when it becomes spiritual. At more than just a glance, right before each and every one of us the Lord is smiling inside of the holy spirit, leaning forward, and very happy indeed. A huge whirling white light is hanging over His head right now. From big to bigger, but more in the upper realm, where a long beam of white penetrates the Lord from the bottom of His feet to the very top of His golden crown which is shining. By the way, the Lord is relaxing. The white light has thickened itself through the Lord's face. Hard to believe He helps so much with telling us the tale. Let our mind be at ease. The whirling creates long white locks of hair upon the Lord's head, falling down to His shoulders. His beard and mustache turned white and seemed to have changed dramatically from the whirling white light.

Waiting for Him to change. Now that white light is smoother across the Lord's forehead, the glowing shows His mustache and beard have turned brown again. Jesus has very nice long brown hair, too, which He revealed having a small flipping curl at the very bottom.

You can disapprove all you want, but the Lord changes to braided hair now, and appeared ladylike, facially. But have faith, God probably did that on purpose. A large gold star shines upon the Lord's left knee. And a golden star is glowing softly upon His whole face. There's a silver cross which He wears on His left hand, forth finger. A closed fist revealed that. He is normal looking again. What God does with Jesus is for the best. He loves Him very much.

Funny kids again, and here they are. Four white lights brought into view those adorable babies, not more than a year old they are moving about with help from the Lord. Those lights are attached to their whirling white light buggy rides. Shaped exactly the same, you'll find it very amusing how cute they look, not tucked in, but holding on with their curling hands filled with bits of cotton like clouds. Not to make fun of anyone, but the group of kids have cloudy white halos which are gradually whirling about around the top of their heads. They could all be girls with "light" bonnets. Each buggy made to be as the whirling white light ride in heaven have lined up with each other, whereas their lights send a glowing beam ahead of them to the next petite child. Whatever it is the Lord, Father God, and what the Virgin Mary brings us inside of their spiritual world called "heaven" we shall enjoy. They wish that we try a little tenderness in our daily life. That's a good idea. They wonder a little bit about the way we act. So they say. Come to find out an angel well-proportioned swooped on in from the light, and suddenly lifted. The wings are quite a golden white mix, but there is some sort of dimming going on with the color. In heaven, there is no such thing as less color, right? Depending on the extent to the situation God has us in, that could differ then. Beautiful, very much so. The angel is that of a charming brown haired lady. She wears three gold stars inside of her hair. Actually through her thick dark strands each star gleams bright, and they even form an arch. One star centered inside of her bangs. She does have a soft glowing white halo, not at all blinding. A new friend was brought up into the spirit world is why she is here visiting. First just a ball of white light for a face, and then a woman's features comes through the light, that human being who she brought forward to see the Lord. Two grave markers are at a forty-five degree angle. The lady angel in the light feels a death was noted, and with the assistance of her Lord, angelic wings were provided. She was able to assist an earthly soul join them in heaven, as it was the woman's time to be celebrated with her Maker up above. Not to make the gravestones seem so grey and gloomy, the spirit of God and the Lord have thrown in a very decorative background to the markers. Many of the red, white and yellow balloons drift slowly within their eternal presence of a heavenly spirit. But wait, there is much more to say. A small yellow heart along side of a white and the red one appeared.

What a joy to commemorate our Lord when we are brought to Him. When He celebrates with us in full glory we will feel everything that is right with the Lord inside of His heart. He will make us feel very tall indeed. It looks like the whirling white light ride in heaven was passed over with the lady who just went on to be with the Lord, or was it? The angel and the woman were inside of a soothing white light, but if it wasn't whirling beneath them that's fine. However, if the angelic lady who just helped raise the woman up from the dead did enjoy the peaceful ride with her inside of the white light, heaven gave them the most exciting thrill ever to be known. That would be greater than being great. Knowing one thing for sure they both had a look of awe expressed on their face. The heavens have opened.